THE
PERFECT
COC...

THE PERFECT COCKTAIL

Hints, Tips, and Recipes from a Master Bartender

GREG DEMPSEY

MAIN STREET BOOKS

DOUBLEDAY New York London Toronto Sydney Auckland

A Main Street Book

PUBLISHED BY DOUBLEDAY

a division of Bantam Doubleday Dell
Publishing Group, Inc.
1540 Broadway, New York, New York 10036

MAIN STREET BOOKS, DOUBLEDAY, and the
portrayal of a building with a tree are trademarks of
Doubleday, a division of Bantam Doubleday Dell
Publishing Group, Inc.

Book design by Gretchen Achilles
Illustrations © 1995 by Diana Jensen

Library of Congress Cataloging-in-Publication Data

Dempsey, Greg, 1969–
    The perfect cocktail : hints, tips, and recipes from a
master bartender / Greg Dempsey.
        p.   cm.
    "A Main Street book."
    1. Bartending—Handbooks, manuals, etc.   I. Title.
TX951.D42   1995
641.8'74—dc20   95-18953
                                                  CIP

ISBN 0-385-47914-X

10 9 8 7 6 5 4 3

CONTENTS

FOREWORD

The Perfect Cocktail does what no other guide to bartending accomplishes. Oddly enough, it explains how to bartend. Other guides do little more than simply list drinks. *The Perfect Cocktail* has put the focus where it should be: on the nuts and bolts of bartending. After all, a bartender, like a chef, must know more than just the recipes to succeed in his or her profession. *The Perfect Cocktail* explains every aspect of bartending from the most significant points to the smallest details; no aspect of bartending is left untouched.

Many other guides claim to be the official guides to bartending. For many reasons they are not. *The Perfect Cocktail* is an invaluable tool for the home bartender, the beginning bartender, and the established professional. It teaches the aspiring bartender the tricks of the old pro, yet is a great reference for the seasoned pro. *The Perfect Cocktail* was written by a bartender, not a writer, and for this reason it has all the information that is pertinent to the trade, without the fluff.

The problems with other bartending guides are many. Here are a few of the most common:

- Most other guides contain obsolete, and often incorrect, ingredients.

- Most other guides contain incorrect quantities.

- Many of the other guides contain far too many drink recipes, making them cumbersome reference tools.

- In most other guides, the important and demanding skill of making mixed shots is overlooked.

Let's look at a few of the differences between this guide and the other guides on the market. Many bartending books frequently have obsolete ingredients but *The Perfect Cocktail* includes modern ingredients. For example, most other guides have yet to replace recipes using lemon juice and powdered sugar with the modern-day equivalent found in every bar in the land, sour mix.

Incorrect quantities is another common problem with the other guides. Most other guides, including the self-proclaimed "official bartender's guide," Mr. Boston, has as its main ingredient for a Fuzzy Navel, 3 ounces of peach schnapps. In most bars throughout America, pouring 3 ounces of peach schnapps would constitute a double or a triple Fuzzy Navel, and would probably get anyone who poured that amount fired. A Fuzzy Navel does not call for 3 ounces of peach schnapps, in fact it does not call for any ounces, but rather a shot. A shot is an unregulated amount, usually somewhere between $3/4$ ounce to $1^1/2$ ounces, but each bar determines its own shot. The fact that the size of a shot is different for every bar is another important point which other guides fail to recognize. *The Perfect Cocktail* refers to all liquor (except wine) with respect to a "shot" not an ounce. After all, this is the language of the bartender.

Any bartender knows that although there are

thousands of drink recipes, there are only around fifty or sixty mixed drinks which are ever ordered. The other guides include hundreds, and in some cases thousands of useless drink recipes while lacking a section with just the most popular drinks. This guide includes plenty of fun drinks to make at home, as well as a comprehensive list of those most-ordered drinks. This chapter on America's most popular drinks will help the beginning bartender with easy reference to the bread and butter drinks. *The Perfect Cocktail* is designed to be a quick reference tool to be used behind the bar, not a large and clumsy dictionary of drinks that sits in the corner of the bar collecting dust.

It should be noted that there are many discrepancies with regard to drink recipes, especially those recipes for mixed shots. These discrepancies probably exist because other guides have neglected the importance of the shot. In fact, most do not even contain recipes for mixed shots. Discrepancies over drink recipes are most apparent between regions of the country. However, differences may also exist between bars and even between bartenders in the same bar. *The Perfect Cocktail* has made every attempt to use the most widely accepted recipes for each drink or shot. It is *The Perfect Cocktail*'s purpose to bridge this gap and become the undisputed authority on drink recipes.

Mixed shots are the most demanding part of modern-day bartending. So *The Perfect Cocktail* includes a section devoted to this facet of bartending, something which is absent in most other guides. *The Perfect Cocktail* gives you the ingredients for a great number of these shots and the instructions in the difficult and often nerve-racking task of making them. This guide has included over a hundred recipes for mixed shots because, unlike mixed drinks, patrons will often give a description of the type of shot he or she wishes to try and allow the bartender to use his or her discretion in choosing a shot to fit the description.

Finally, and as important as any of the points above, this guide gives the aspiring bartender the basic knowledge to succeed in this often-demanding profession. Unlike other guides in this field, *The Perfect Cocktail* gives the aspiring bartender short-cuts and tricks of the trade for behind-the-bar success. In short, *The Perfect Cocktail* makes bartending easy to learn.

BARTENDER'S RESPONSIBILITY

If misused, alcohol can be very dangerous. Drunken driving is the most serious problem relating to alcohol. It is by far the leading cause of automobile fatalities in the United States today, accounting for nearly half of all highway deaths. For this reason, bartenders should monitor the alcohol consumption of their customers and guests.

THE SIX GENERAL DRINK CATEGORIES

The Perfect Cocktail has created a classification system to better aid in explaining how to make mixed drinks. This new system classifies drinks into six general categories. The categories are not determined by how drinks are mixed, the basis of the old system, but rather on a combination of these factors: quantity of liquor added to the drink, number of liquors added and whether combined with mixer/s, and whether or not the drink is served with ice.

1. ONE-LIQUOR DRINKS

One-liquor drinks obviously have only one liquor and usually require just one shot of that liquor, unless otherwise requested (i.e., a double vodka and tonic).

EXAMPLES:

RUM AND COKE
- 1 shot rum
- Cola

Serve.

SCREWDRIVER
- 1 shot vodka
- Orange juice

Serve.

2. TWO-LIQUOR DRINKS

Two-liquor drinks require a combined total of between a shot and a shot and a half of two liquors. This combination is not necessarily equal parts of both liquors. For instance, a White Russian calls for more vodka than Kahlúa. When making a two-liquor drink on the rocks, it is important to have a full glass of ice because it will make the drink appear larger when in fact it is a small drink, though quite a lot of liquor. Because of the additional liquor, two-liquor drinks are more expensive than those drinks containing just a shot.

EXAMPLES:

MANHATTAN
- 1 shot American whiskey
- ½ shot sweet vermouth

Stir and garnish with a cherry.

WHITE RUSSIAN
- 1 shot vodka
- ½ shot coffee-flavored liqueur (Kahlúa)
- Cream

Shake.

3. MULTI-LIQUOR DRINKS

Multi-liquor drinks require a combined total of approximately two full shots of three or more liquors. These drinks can be difficult to make when you begin bartending, but with practice you should get the hang of pouring them. Remember: due to the greater amount of alcohol in multi-liquor drinks, these drinks will be more expensive than one- and two-liquor drinks.

EXAMPLES:

ALABAMA SLAMMER

- ³/₄ shot amaretto
- ³/₄ shot Southern Comfort
- Splash of sloe gin
- Orange juice
- Pineapple juice

Stir.

LONG ISLAND ICED TEA

- ½ shot vodka
- ½ shot gin
- ½ shot rum
- ½ shot tequila
- Splash of triple sec
- Sour mix
- Splash of cola

Garnish with a lemon slice and serve.

4. ON THE ROCKS

On-the-rocks drinks, often referred to as simply "rocks," require a small rocks glass filled with ice and a combined shot and a half of the desired liquor, liqueur, or denoted mixer. The term "on the rocks" not only means on ice, but more importantly a shot and a half of the combined ingredients. Because some people hear the term "on the rocks" and think it only means "on ice," you may have to enlighten them to the increased amount of liquor. When making an on-the-rocks drink it is important to *fill* the glass with ice. If the glass is not completely filled with ice a drink served on the rocks will look as if the bartender underpoured the drink. It will appear this way because an on-the-rocks drink has only a shot and a half of combined ingredients. This may be a lot of liquor, but it is not a lot of liquid, and will look very small even in a small rocks glass.

Note: Today, many of the drinks that originate as shots are being ordered on the rocks (i.e., Sex on the Beach, Russian Quaalude, etc.), and for this reason it is a good idea to ask patrons whether they would like the drink as a shot or on the rocks.

EXAMPLES:

SCOTCH
- ½ shots Scotch whisky
Serve.

RUSSIAN QUAALUDE
- ½ shot Stolichnaya (Russian vodka)
- ½ shot hazelnut liqueur (Frangelico)
- ½ shot amaretto
Serve.

5. STRAIGHT UP

Sometimes shortened to "up." This category of drinks calls for a shot and a half of the desired liquor or liqueur served without ice in either a brandy snifter or a cocktail/Martini glass. Drinks ordered "straight up" may or may not be chilled; those which are chilled are similar to on-the-rocks drinks but are served in a different glass and without ice. If chilling is required, do so in a shaker and strain into a cocktail glass. If requested unchilled (almost always either a brandy or a straight liqueur), pour straight into a brandy snifter.

EXAMPLES:

GRAND MARNIER
- 1½ shots Grand Marnier

MARTINI
REQUESTED "STRAIGHT UP"

- 1½ shots gin
- Splash of dry vermouth
- Desired garnish

Strain from shaker with ice into cocktail glass. Garnish.

6. SHOTS

Because shots are the most discretionary aspect of the bar business, the size of a shot will vary from bar to bar. Shots range anywhere from ¾ ounce to around 1½ ounces (rarely larger). The given bar's management will determine the size of the shot. This is why *The Perfect Cocktail* deals with all alcohol in terms of shots, not ounces. Straight shots require a total of one shot of a given liquor or liqueur. Mixed shots require different liquors, liqueurs, and mixers combined for a total of one shot.

EXAMPLES:

WHISKEY
(STRAIGHT OR NEAT SHOT)

- 1 shot whiskey

B-52 (MIXED SHOT)

- ⅓ shot coffee-flavored liqueur (Kahlúa)
- ⅓ shot Irish cream
- ⅓ shot Grand Marnier

Layer.

THE THREE WAYS
TO MIX A DRINK

THE HIGHBALL

The mixing of a highball is done directly in the glass that will be served to customers. Today many drinks originally intended to be served in the highball or large rocks glass, including most drinks containing carbonated mixers, are generally served in the small rocks glass.* The highball is the easiest drink to mix: simply add the drink's ingredients into the glass and serve. There is a chronological process which should be followed in making any highball.

The first step in creating a drink is choosing the proper glass for the designated drink and filling it with ice. Unless ordered "straight up," all drinks are served with a full glass of ice. The full glass of ice is not only to keep the drink cold, but also to give the drink a stronger taste of alcohol. If the drink does not begin with a full glass of ice, the drink will require a greater amount of mixer to fill the glass, the alcohol will be too diluted, and it will therefore taste like a weaker drink. Weak-tasting drinks translate into unhappy customers and lower tips.

The second step is adding the different ingredients to the glass. As might be expected, this is the part of making a mixed drink which requires the

*This is probably because bars realized they could increase the number of drinks they serve and decrease the amount of mixers they go through by serving most highballs in the small rocks glass.

most skill. The addition of liquor should be very exact. To add the proper amount of liquor, use either a jigger or free pour (see section on "Free Pouring," page 17).

The addition of mixer is less exact. If there is only one mixer (like Coke in a Rum and Coke), it is added after the liquor and should fill the remainder of the glass. To avoid spillage, you should fill to about half an inch from the rim of the glass. If there are two primary mixers as in a Bay Breeze (orange juice and cranberry juice), equal parts of each are added. This guide does not place measurements next to most primary mixers. This is because primary mixers should fill the glass after the liquor has been poured. With two primary mixers, the first mixer fills the remainder of the glass halfway, the second mixer fills the glass to the top.

Examples of secondary mixers, such as Rose's lime juice, grenadine, or Tabasco, make up only a small part of a drink. In most cases, secondary mixers can be added either before or after primary mixers. Secondary mixers are usually strong-tasting, and therefore should be added sparingly. These measurements will usually be either a dash (less than a teaspoon) or a splash (a little less than ½ an ounce).

After the addition of the various mixers the drink is ready for the garnish. Depending on the garnish and if time permits, give it a squeeze and drop it into the drink. Complete the drink by adding a straw or mixing rod, and serve.

THE CHRONOLOGICAL ORDER IN THE MAKING OF A MIXED DRINK

1.   Garnish the rim of the glass, usually with salt or sugar (this is only done on a handful of drinks).

2. Fill the designated glass with ice.

3. Pour the primary liquor into the glass.

4. Pour the secondary liquor into the glass.

5. Pour the primary mixers into the glass (in most cases steps 5 and 6 are interchangeable; however, certain drinks require step 6 to follow step 5).

6. Pour the secondary mixers into the glass.

7. Add the garnish to the glass.

8. Add a straw or mixing rod to the drink.

9. Serve with a coaster or napkin.

When more than one drink is ordered at the same time it will speed the process considerably if the bartender makes the drinks simultaneously. This is done by lining up the glasses as close to each other as possible, then adding ice to those glasses which require it. Drinks having common ingredients should be made next to each other. For example, if the drink order calls for two Vodka and Tonics, a Gin and Tonic, a Screwdriver, and a Bourbon on the Rocks, the bartender should line up four small rocks glasses followed by a large rocks glass, all to be filled with ice. The bartender begins by pouring a shot and a half of bourbon into the first rocks glass, the Bourbon on the Rocks is now complete. The bartender then pours a shot of gin into the next small rocks glass. He or she is now ready to proceed to the remaining drinks, which call for vodka. A shot of vodka should be poured into each of the remaining glasses, one into each of the small rocks glasses and one into the large rocks glass. It is now time for the mixers. First fill the three glasses in the middle, the Gin and Tonic and the two Vodka and Tonics, with tonic water. Now fill the large rocks glass with orange juice to complete the Screwdriver. Garnish the tonic drinks with lime wedges. Add mixing rods to the drinks served in the small rocks glasses and a straw to the Screwdriver served in the large rocks glass. Finally, serve the drinks. This method has no wasted time or tasks. Each bottle and mixer is pulled out and used only once. At first, mixing a number of drinks at the same time will be confusing, but with practice it will come naturally.

SHAKEN AND STIRRED DRINKS

In the past, the making of shaken and stirred drinks was a practice that was strictly adhered to. Today, though making a small comeback in certain areas, the practice has been all but abandoned by many bars and bartenders. Today, the only way to assure that a drink originally intended to be shaken or stirred will be mixed as such is if it is ordered "straight up, chilled." Of course, one can still order a drink "shaken" or "stirred."

There are several reasons for the move away from shaken and stirred drinks. The first reason for abandoning this practice is because of the public's shift from the straight-up cocktail to the on-the-rocks drink. Now most drinks originally intended to be served in a cocktail glass "straight up, chilled" are overwhelmingly ordered "on the rocks," most notably by the younger crowd. This change in tastes is probably because a drink over ice is not as strong as a drink straight up; the ice dilutes the mix, weakening the drink. Today's preference for on-the-rocks drinks means that it is not as important to shake or stir a drink, but it is a skill every bartender should know. The main reason for shaking or stirring a drink was in fact not for mixing, but rather for chilling. Because most drinks originally intended to be shaken or stirred are today served on the rocks, no outside chilling is needed. However, it is essential to know how to mix a straight up, chilled drink. The final reason that shaking and stirring drinks has been neglected is that in busier bars where time is short,

---

pouring drinks as if each were a highball, needing no mixing, saves valuable time, thus allowing the bar and bartender to make more money. Though these mixing practices have declined in recent years, it is important to know how to perform each act. The drink recipes in this book denote the intended mixing technique for each drink.

THE SHAKEN DRINK

To shake a drink the same guidelines are used as for making a highball, except that the ice and ingredients are not added directly to the glass the drink is served in, but rather they are added to a mixing glass used in conjunction with a metal tumbler. Pour the mix into the mixing glass because it is smaller and will fit into the large metal tumbler, and mix. Unless mixing many drinks, I recommend that you not measure drinks in a tumbler because it may contain too much liquid for the serving glass to handle. After adding the ingredients into the mixing glass, secure the mouth of the tumbler over the mouth of the mixing glass firmly pressing it to form a water-tight seal. You just made a "shaker." Hold both components of the shaker together and shake it in an up-and-down motion, making sure the mix goes back and forth between both mixing glass and tumbler. Now place the shaker down, the tumbler facing up, and break the seal which has been created by hitting the tumbler with the butt of your hand. Remove the mixing glass and strain the contents of the tumbler into either a cocktail glass or a small rocks glass with or without ice.

Though most bartenders only shake drinks served straight up, you may be asked to shake a drink ordered "on the rocks." The most efficient way to do this is to use a short shaker. A short shaker allows you to shake the drink using the glass it will be served in, thereby eliminating the straining of the drink as well as excess glasses to be cleaned. Simply place the short shaker over the intended glass containing the mix, shake the drink, then simply remove the metal tumbler, garnish the drink, and serve. Don't forget to clean the shaker after using it.

The rule of thumb for knowing when to shake drinks is to do so when a drink has a large number of ingredients, because they will need shaking to properly mix. You should also shake drinks that have ingredients that don't easily mix, such as cream or sour mix.

THE STIRRED DRINK

A stirred drink can either be made in the glass it will be served in, if it will be served on the rocks, or added to a tumbler first if requested "straight up." If a drink is ordered "on the rocks" it is faster to stir it in the glass in which it will be served, and this will not create excess instruments to be cleaned. To make a stirred drink, simply add the required ingredients to the glass, stir the drink once or twice with the mixing rod, and serve. For stirred drinks which are ordered "straight up," combine the ingredients in the tumbler and stir the mix with either a long bar spoon or a long mixing rod. Some bartenders will swirl the tumbler in a circular motion to mix and chill the drink. Though this is not technically correct, it is faster, and to most drinkers the difference in style goes unnoticed. The drink is now ready to be strained from the tumbler into a cocktail glass, garnished, and served.

POURING LIQUOR

Possibly the most important part of bartending is pouring liquor. The bartender must pour the correct amount of liquor in each drink. An old bartender saying is, "Short neither the house nor the customer." In other words, pour the exact amount ordered.

USING A JIGGER

The beginning bartender should use a jigger until he or she is an accurate free pourer. The jigger will regulate the amount of liquor you pour. Because bars use different shot sizes, there are different sized jiggers depending upon the bar you work in. Each bar should have only those jiggers which will properly regulate its specification of a shot.

To keep customers happy, only fill the jigger about three quarters full before pouring the shot into the glass. Then while pouring the three-quarters full jigger into the glass, continue pouring the remaining quarter of the shot directly into the glass; this amount is so small you can eyeball it or use a count (see below). Doing this will give the customer the illusion that he or she is receiving a generous pour when in actuality only a shot is being dispensed.

In time, and if allowed by the "house" (the bar), a bartender will graduate from using the jigger and move up to free pouring. Free pouring will save the bartender valuable time, and it also looks more professional. To free pour accurately, one must be able to pour a given amount of liquor (i.e., shot, shot and a half, double) without using a jigger. To accomplish this a bartender uses a count. A count depends on two factors: the rate of flow of the speedpourer (this is a device which is placed over the mouth of the bottle and regulates the flow of liquid); how fast the bartender silently counts. The brand or model of the speedpourer must never change or the count will have to be altered to the rate of flow of the new pourer. It is also important that the bartender always hold the bottle at the same spot, the neck of the bottle, and when pouring hold the bottle completely upside down. Place all speedpourers facing away from the label of the bottle to which each is affixed, so that when pouring, customers can read the label. Then place each bottle in the speed rack with its speedpourer facing forward. The spout of the speedpourer is normally angled, so in order to get an even flow of liquor the speedpourer must face forward. The second factor is completely subjective. Count at whatever rate you desire, but you must be consistent. Your consistency will determine your precision at pouring exactly a shot every time. Most bartenders count in their head using numbers, which is what I recommend, yet anything can be used as a count, including letters, words, or whatever. *The Perfect Cocktail* recommends a four count for a shot. A four-count shot means each count is equal to a quarter shot. Using a four-count mode, a two count would be half a shot, a six count would be a shot and a half, and an eight count would be a double.

To determine your count, fill an empty liquor bottle with water and place a speedpourer over its mouth. Then practice your count while trying to pour a perfect shot into a jigger or shot glass. You will most likely have to adjust your count to coincide with the rate at which the shot is poured. Remember, a shot's size is dependent upon the bar in which it is poured, therefore use a jigger or shot glass which represents the size shot which your bar endorses. If there is no speed pourer, the flow of liquor will be unregulated, and you will have to measure liquor with a jigger or a shot glass. With practice, an aspiring bartender should be able to free pour efficiently in very little time. The beginning free pourer may have trouble keeping count the first few nights in which he or she is busy. If this is the case, simply revert to using the jigger until you feel comfortable free pouring in a pressure situation.

MIXED SHOTS, SPECIALTY SHOTS, SHOOTERS OR SHOTS

Mixed shots are a difficult and demanding part of bartending. Success in making shots will only come with practice. Shots that are layered or served unchilled are relatively easy to make because they are poured directly into the shot glass. The difficulty in making shots that are chilled in a shaker is in knowing the correct amount of ingredients to add to the mix, because there is no glass regulating the amount of mix to add. Because *The Perfect Cocktail* gives its shot ingredients in fractions of a shot, simply multiply the fraction by the number of shots to be made in order to arrive at the proper quantity. For example, if a group of people ordered five Alabama Slammer shots, each of the five ingredients in the mix calls for a fifth of a shot, therefore one shot of each of the five ingredients would be called for to complete the order. That was easy. Let's say there were seven shots ordered for the same shot, a more difficult calculation. In this instance we know that a total of seven shots will be needed. We also know that each of the five ingredients makes up one part of the shot, therefore we will need a little over $1\frac{1}{4}$ and a little under $1\frac{1}{2}$ shots per ingredient. There is no time to get out your calculator; this is where your eye, your intuition, your bartending skill, and maybe even a little luck come in handy. Simply wing it. It is important to relax when making shots. They can be difficult to create, but take comfort in knowing that because they are consumed or "shot down" so fast and are so small (only around an ounce), it is very difficult to distinguish a problem with a shot unless you really screwed up the recipe. In time and with practice you will gain the ability to efficiently complete the requested shot order.

The majority of mixed shots call for chilling. When making chilled shots fill your shaker with ice followed by the shot's ingredients. After the mix has been shaken in the shaker it is ready to be poured. At this time, line up the correct number of shot glasses for the order in a tight row. Each shot glass should be touching the glass next to it (see illustration). If the glasses are touching each other, the pouring process will be more efficient, allowing you to continue pouring while going from one shot glass to the next. You are now ready to dispense the shots from the shaker.

If using a Boston shaker, which consists of a metal tumbler and a mixing glass, and if the shot order is small enough, dispense the shots from the mixing glass instead of the tumbler. Using the mixing glass will allow you to see the mix through the glass while pouring the shots. Place the strainer over the mouth of the mixing glass or the tumbler and begin pouring at one end of the row of shot glasses. Work toward the opposite end filling each glass approximately half full with the mix. When you reach the opposite end, fill the final glass ap-

proximately three quarters full and then work back toward the end which you began. This second pass should find each half-full shot glass being filled an additional quarter, so when this second pass is complete each shot glass will be approximately three quarters full. With each glass three quarters full, if you run out of mix at this time the glasses are sufficiently full to allow them to be served. However, if there is more mix in the shaker, make another pass or two until the shaker is empty or all of the shot glasses are full. Because estimating the correct amount of ingredients to add when making multiple shots is difficult, we recommend this technique to allow for some degree of error in the quantity of the mix. We do not suggest pouring one glass after another until each is filled. The problem with this method is that when you arrive at the last glass there may be no mix left or only enough to fill it part way. The drink order will be much more attractive and professional looking if each glass is equally full.

LAYERED DRINKS

Some drinks, most notably shots and poussecafés (multi-liqueur drinks, best served in a cordial glass), are designed to be layered. Layering is when a drink's ingredients are poured so that they are layered one on top of the other, like oil and water. This is done to make the drink taste and look better. Recipes for layered drinks are always given in the correct order for layering. The rule of thumb for layering is always to pour the heaviest liquor first followed by lighter and lightest liquors. However, just pouring the ingredients in correct order is not always enough to produce a successful drink. To help in the layering process the liquor is poured gently over the back side of a spoon, which slows and spreads the flow of the liquor, keeping it from mixing with the heavier liquors already in the glass. If there isn't a spoon handy or there isn't enough time, pour the liquors in a slow and careful manner.

Floating is a form of layering in which only the top liquor is layered, and is often done with mixed drinks. To float an ingredient on top of a drink (in a Harvey Wallbanger, Galliano is floated), simply pour the liquor slowly and carefully into the glass. It  is best if you pour over ice already in the glass at the top of the drink. The ice will stop the downward flow of the liquor, keeping the given liquor from mixing with those ingredients already in the glass.

FLAMING ALCOHOL

Before you serve flaming alcohol make sure that the bar permits this practice. When flaming alcohol at home, make sure not to flame near curtains, draperies, paper, or anything else which is flammable. Depending on the proof of the liquor, you may have to warm the alcohol so that it will light. Liquors with proofs over 100 don't need to be warmed prior to flaming.

There are several basic safety rules you need to abide by when flaming drinks. Never flame alcohol in a bright room or in the daylight. Flames from alcohol are nearly invisible in a bright room, so you should only flame in a dark room where you can keep track of the flame in case there is a spill. Never use large amounts of alcohol to flame drinks. A good technique for flaming drinks is to warm a teaspoon of liquor, ignite it, then slowly pour the flaming liquor into the prepared drink. This is safer and easier than lighting the liquor right in the glass. Never pour liquor from a bottle into a flaming dish or drink, because the flame may travel up the stream and into the bottle. Keep flaming alcohol at arm's distance, as it may shoot up from the glass or dish at any time. I also advise avoiding flaming liquor on nights in which the bar is very busy; it is possible a patron could accidentally be pushed into the bar, spilling the flaming drink.

If someone requests a flamed drink, the safest are the Lemon Drop shot and the Cordless Screwdriver. Flaming either of these shots is optional and can be done by pouring a splash of 151-proof rum over the slice of lemon or orange. Ignite the slice which sits atop the shot glass and view the flame. The flame will be short-lived but will present little danger. To ensure safety, any other drink that is flamed should be extinguished prior to drinking. This can be done effectively by covering the top of the glass, eliminating the supply of oxygen. Place a damp napkin in the palm of your hand and quickly cover the top of the glass with it.

FROZEN DRINKS

Making frozen drinks is another part of bartending that is often difficult for the beginner. The reason is that frozen drinks are not made in the glass they are served in, but rather in a blender. A trick for new bartenders is to combine the ingredients directly in the glass in which the drink will be served, then pour the contents of the glass into the blender. Doing this will insure that the right amount of mix is added to the blender. After you have had some experience in making frozen drinks, you should be able to gauge how high the blender should be filled for one or more frozen drinks.

If a frozen drink order comes in along with several other drinks, make the frozen drink first. This will give you ample time to work on the rest of the order during the "dead" time while the drink is being blended.

To make a frozen drink, first add the shot of primary liquor followed by the secondary liquor (if called for). At this point add the mix or fruit. Next, add any secondary mixers. Finally, add approximately one cup of ice (8 ounces). This amount as well as the amount of mixers added will depend on the size of the glass in which the drink will be served. Remember, bar glasses come in all different sizes, so add ice to the blender accordingly. The mix is now ready for blending. If it is an especially thick mix, you may want to start the blender on low speed, and as the mixture becomes more viscous adjust it to high. The drink should be blended in fifteen to forty seconds, depending on several variables including room temperature, the temperature of the mix, the power and speed of the blender, and the sharpness of the blade. With time, you will be able to gauge all of the above variables. A rule of thumb for blending is that the drink is usually about done when the condensation on the outside of the blender reaches the height of the mix within the blender. After the drink is done blending, it should have about the same consistency (or just a bit thicker) than that of a convenience-store Slurpee. For a slushier drink, simply add more ice. The drink is now ready to be poured, garnished, and served.

Making multiple frozen drinks is very similar to making multiple chilled shots. In both, the beginning bartender may find it difficult to add the right amount of ingredients to the mix, especially when making a large order. Therefore, the pouring technique for making chilled shots should also be utilized when making multiple frozen drinks. If you haven't made enough mix for a three-drink order—something which can happen to even a veteran bartender—you will have a problem if you fill the first two glasses and only have enough to fill the third glass halfway. Being half a glass short and balancing it out over three glasses is fine.

GARNISHES

The first thing a bartender should do when he or she starts a shift is to make sure that there are enough garnishes, and if there are not, to cut enough to last the night. Garnishing a drink is the easiest part of making a drink. All you really need to know to properly garnish a drink is how to cut the garnishes. Cutting garnishes is part of the daily routine for a bartender. The garnishes which require cutting are limes, lemons, and oranges. All other garnishes are simply placed, as is, into the drink.

Limes:
These are cut in half and then into wedges (quarters or thirds of the original half cut). Squeeze the garnish over the drink then drop into the drink. If you have ample time, rub the lime around the rim of the glass, it will add extra flavor to the drink.

Lemons and Oranges:
These are cut in half and then sliced four to five times perpendicular to the original half cut. Some bartenders place a small incision in the middle of the fruit so it can straddle the rim of the drink; this is

optional. Oranges are simply squeezed over the drink then dropped in the drink. Lemons are either squeezed over the drink then dropped in, or requested as a "twist." If a twist of lemon is requested, the meat is removed from a portion of the peel and discarded. The portion of peel should be at least an inch long by approximately a quarter inch wide. This piece, referred to as a "twist," is then twisted over the drink and dropped into it. If time permits, rub the twist over the rim of the glass; this will impart more of the peel's flavor to the drink.

Celery Stalks:
These simply need to be cleaned prior to placing in the drink; they are most frequently added to Bloody Marys.

Maraschino Cherries:
These are added to a drink straight from the jar.

Green Pitted Olives and Cocktail Onions:

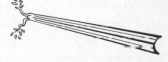

These are rarely used in anything but Martinis. They are added straight from the jar. A Martini with a cocktail onion is called a Gibson.

It should be noted that on a busy night a bartender will not have time to squeeze every piece of fruit prior to dropping it into the drink.

Large Rocks or Highball Glass.

(10–12 ounces): Always filled with ice, this glass is used for serving most drinks that contain fruit juice or sour mix as primary mixers. The large rocks glass is the most versatile glass. It is used for serving all soft drinks and can be used interchangeably with the Collins glass. The large rocks or highball glass is also used if someone orders a tall drink, for instance a tall Rum and Coke, which is normally served in a small rocks glass.

Small Rocks or Old-Fashioned Glass

(6–10 ounces): Always filled with ice, this glass is used for serving most drinks that contain cola and other sodas, tonic water, water, cream, and sometimes juices as its primary mixers. A small rocks glass is also used for all drinks ordered "on the rocks."

Collins Glass

(10–14 ounces): This glass is used for all drinks ordered "Collins" (desired liquor, sour mix, splash of soda, and a cherry). The Collins glass is also used on select other drinks. The Collins glass is basically interchangeable with the large rocks glass, however it is not as prevalent as the large rocks glass.

Cocktail or Martini Glass

(3–6 ounces): This glass is used for drinks ordered "straight up, chilled" and is most closely associated with the Martini served straight up. If time permits, always chill the cocktail glass before serving a drink in it. The stem of the cocktail glass is to be held by the drinker so as not to warm the contents of the glass. The frappé is the only drink which calls for ice, shaved or crushed, to be added to a cocktail glass.

Whiskey Sour Glass

(4–8 ounces): This glass is used primarily for "sours" (desired liquor, sour mix, a cherry, and a lemon slice) served straight up, chilled. Most other drinks served in sour glasses contain sour mix as their primary mixer.

Brandy Snifter

(Snifter) (4–24 ounces): This glass is used for serving brandy and liqueurs requested "straight up, unchilled" (straight-up liqueurs can also be served in a cordial glass). The body of the snifter is designed to be held by the palm of the hand, thus warming the snifter's contents.

Shot Glass

(¾–2 ounces): The shot glass is used exclusively for serving shots.

Cordial

(1–1½ ounces): This glass, sometimes referred to as a "pony," is used for serving liqueurs or cordials straight up. The cordial is most often used for after-dinner drinks.

Irish Coffee Cup

(8–12 ounces): This cup is used for serving all hot drinks.

Margarita Glass

(8–14 ounces): This goblet is used for serving frozen drinks, most notably the Frozen Margarita. Margarita glasses are expensive and fragile; for these reasons they are not found behind most bars.

Beer Mug

(10–16 ounces): The mug is the most informal of all beer glasses. The mug is the best glass to chill because its thickness enables it to stay cold longer than any other glass.

Pilsner Glass

(10–14 ounces): This is the most formal beer glass. Because of its fragile nature, this glass is seldom found in bars, but many microbreweries and upscale restaurants have them.

Pint Glass

(14–16 ounces): Today's popular pint glass is a misnomer, in actuality it is usually less than 16 ounces (⁷/₈ of a pint to a pint). It is found at most bars and is used for premium draft beer including ales, porters, and stouts. Due to the popularity of this glass, many bars are beginning to serve more than just beer in the pint glass; in some instances it is being used in place of the large rocks glass.

White Wine Glass

(10–14 ounces): This glass is used for serving white wines and is usually taller than the red wine glass (it has a longer stem, but a smaller lip and bowl).

Red Wine Glass

(12–16 ounces): This glass has a large lip and a large bowl to enable the drinker to experience the aroma and body of the red wine.

Champagne Flute

(6–10 ounces): This glass is used for serving champagne, sparkling wine, and a select few other drinks. The tall and slender glass is designed to show off the wine's sparkling bubbles. Most bars stock only a few of these fragile glasses, because champagne is rarely ordered except for New Year's Eve, at which time most bars serve champagne in less-expensive plastic flutes.

Punch Cup

(6–8 ounces): This glass is generally not found behind bars, but rather at parties where eggnog and punch are served.

TOOLS OF THE BAR

Jigger/Pony:

This nonregulated measuring instrument is referred to in the bar business simply as a "jigger." Each jigger has two sides, a jigger and a pony. The jigger side is usually ½ ounce larger than the pony side. Jiggers come in several different sizes with the jigger side ranging from 1 to 2 ounces and the pony side ranging in size from ½ to 1 ounce. Generally, nightclubs and large bars catering to a younger crowd will have smaller shots and therefore use a smaller jigger than those of country clubs or bars catering to an older clientele.

Shaker:

This instrument is used for shaking or stirring a drink with ice before pouring it into a serving glass. The Boston shaker is found behind most bars. It is a combination large steel tumbler (about 16 ounces) and smaller mixing glass (about 12 ounces). To begin the process, ice is added to the tumbler followed by the drink's ingredients. A drink that needs stirring before being served straight up, is done so at this time then strained into its proper glass. A drink that needs to be shaken is done so by placing the smaller mixing glass into the tumbler creating a water-tight seal. The drink is shaken a few times and then with the tumbler right side up, the mixing glass is removed from the tumbler. The tumbler now has the entire mix including the ice. A strainer is placed over the mouth of the tumbler and the drink is poured into the glass. Gaining a great deal of popu-

larity is a device called a "short shaker." It saves time when making shaken drinks served on the rocks. The short shaker fits over the mouth of the glass the drink will be served in, therefore allowing the drink to be shaken and served in the same glass.

Strainer:

This porous instrument is used in conjunction with a shaker for pouring straight-up drinks chilled. The strainer is placed over the mouth of the shaker when poured. This allows the drink to flow while holding the ice in the shaker. This instrument is used for making any type of chilled drinks including shots and straight-up drinks.

Speedpourer:

This small plastic or metal device fits over the mouth of a bottle and regulates the flow of the bottle's liquid. If you plan to free pour, this device is a must. When placing a speedpourer on a bottle, make sure the device's spout is perpendicular to the bottle's label. This is important for two reasons: first, if you place each speedpourer accordingly on each bottle and keep it in the speed rack with the device's spout facing forward, you can begin pouring immediately without having to check its positioning (it will not pour at an even rate unless it is positioned correctly); second, placing the speedpourer perpendicular to the label will allow the customer to see the label of the bottle while the bartender pours from the bottle.

Bar Spoon:

This spoon has a long handle (usually at least ten inches long) and is used for mixing drinks in all glasses and tumblers.

Blender:

A must for making frozen and ice-cream drinks, as well as blending fresh fruit. If the blender has a strong motor and sharp blades it can also be used for making shaved ice.

Bartender's Friend:

This handy device has all the different tools needed for opening beer and wine bottles.

Paring Knife:

Used for cutting garnishes and skinning lemons to create a twist. A sharp paring knife is a must behind the bar.

LIQUOR, LIQUEUR, AND MIXERS

Although it is preferable that the bartender have a strong grasp of the different liquors behind the bar, it is not a necessity. The most important knowledge a bartender should have regarding liquor is the category or class of each brand. Often a patron will request the bartender to list the brands of a certain type of liquor the bar carries. For example, many patrons will ask the bartender what kinds of Scotch (whisky) they have. In this instance the bartender should know what brands of Scotch whisky the bar carries (and which it does not!). Liquors that have a strong "brand following" are: brandy, gin, vodka, and all types of whiskey.

DIVISIONS OF LIQUOR

In all bars there are at least two divisions of liquors: "bar" and "call." Many bars have a third division referred to as "top shelf" or "premium." The first and most inexpensive liquor is "bar" or "well." One step up in quality and price from "bar" liquor is "call" liquor, and this is followed by "top shelf" liquor, the finest and most expensive liquor in the house.

BAR OR WELL LIQUOR

This is the "house" or "no-name" liquor, the cheap stuff. It is used whenever a patron makes no distinction as to the brand of liquor he or she desires. Bar or well liquor is almost always found in metal speed racks behind the bar, in front of the bartender. These racks are usually about three feet above the floor. The location of the racks makes the liquor very accessible. The liquor is also arranged in a set order within the racks to make locating the desired bottle as easy as possible. The following liquor is usually present in a speed rack in this order from right to left:

vodka, American whiskey, gin, rum, tequila, triple sec, and Scotch whisky. Other liquors considered "bar," though not usually located in the speed racks because of their infrequent use, are usually located on shelves behind the bar. These would commonly include liqueurs or cordials such as: amaretto, anisette, curaçao, sloe gin, crème de drinks, and schnapps. Remember, the above list of bar liqueurs is not set in stone. Some bars may have one or two of the above liqueurs in the call section.

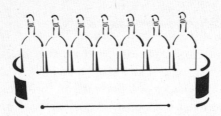

CALL LIQUOR

This is the title given to liquor above bar but below top-shelf liquor in price and quality. Here you will find brand-name American whiskies, mid-range name-brand Scotch whiskies, Irish whiskies, American brandies, most brand-name rums and tequilas, brand-name schnapps such as Rumple Minze, and liqueurs such as Southern Comfort, Jägermeister, and Irish cream. Remember, call and top-shelf liquors are not to be used unless specified by the patron or the drink order.

TOP-SHELF LIQUOR

This class of liquor is proudly displayed behind the bar on attractive, often illuminated, top shelves. The finest and most expensive liquors such as cognac as well as the bar's best bottles of Scotch, vodka, gin, and proprietary liqueurs will be on the top shelf.

The following list contains a concise explanation of the different liquors and their top call brands.

Brandy:

The process used to make brandy is basically the same as that of making whiskey. The difference between the two classes of liquors is that brandy is distilled from fruit while whiskey is derived from grain. Any fruit which is fermented and then distilled is a brandy. The finest brandies are from the Cognac and Armagnac regions of France, although California produces fine brandies as well. Brandy bottles have special labeling to distinguish between the different classes of brandy. For instance, a bottle of brandy with the acronym VSOP on its label describes its contents as Very Special Old Pale. Letters are used in place of words to classify the given bottle. They are:

C—cognac	E—especially
F—fine	O—old
P—pale	S—special
V—very	X—extra

The most popular call brands are: Rémy Martin (Cognac); Hennessy (Cognac); Courvoisier (Cognac); E&J Brandy (American); Christian Brothers (American).

Gin:

This neutral grain spirit is made from juniper berries and an assorted mix of herbs and spices. Gin is normally the second most popular bottle in the speed rack (vodka is the most popular). These two liquors lead the way because they are neutral grain spirits lacking any strong tastes, which make them very mixable. The most popular include Bombay Sapphire, Tanqueray, and Beefeater.

Rum:

First produced in the Caribbean, rum is made from sugar cane and comes in two main classes. *Light rums* are less flavorful and range in color from clear to gold. *Dark rums* are more syrupy and have a richer flavor. Also popular are *flavored rums* like spiced rum and coconut rum. Rum is usually the third most popular bottle in the speed rack. Top-call rums include Myers's (dark), Bacardi (light), Captain Morgan's (spiced), and Malibu (coconut-flavored).

Tequila:

Made in and around the town of Tequila in Mexico, this liquor has gained great popularity over the last twenty-five years. It is made from the *agave tequilana* or blue agave plant. It has a very distinctive, pungent taste. Tequila is a very popular shot and is almost always accompanied with salt and lime (lick salt, drink shot, suck lime), so it's important that you always ask the patron if he or she would like salt and a lime when a tequila shot is ordered. Clear tequilas are usually the bar or well brands. Better tequilas will be darker in color, signifying a longer aging process. Top-call tequilas include José Cuervo and Sauza.

Vodka:

This neutral grain spirit is almost always the most popular "bar" liquor because it can be mixed with almost anything. Although most vodkas have only a smidgen of taste, many today are being produced with mild flavoring, including citrus fruits, pepper, etcetera. Top-call vodkas include Stolichnaya, Tanqueray Sterling, Absolut, and Smirnoff.

Whiskey:

Liquors of this class are made by distilling grains like rye, corn, and barley. Though there are several different classes of whiskies, only origin and consistency will be discussed below. Straight whiskies are those whiskies which are not blended in any way. They are made by one distiller, and because of government regulations are held in bonded warehouses until the barrels of whiskey are bottled. Blended whiskies have no such regulations and, as the name implies, contain the whiskies of two or more distillers blended together. Country of origin is the only other distinction that will be discussed in this book. Each of the four major whiskey-producing countries uses ingredients, distilling processes, even spellings peculiar to its national origin. As a result, each type of whiskey is consumed differently. American and Canadian whiskies are enjoyed neat (straight shots) and are very mixable. Scotch whisky is usually preferred on the rocks or with water, and Irish whiskey is usually enjoyed either on the rocks, as a shot, or with coffee.

AMERICAN WHISKEY: The great majority of this whiskey is distilled in Kentucky, Tennessee, and other bordering states. American whiskey is the most robust of all whiskies, and it is either straight or blended. Of the straight American whiskies there are three major types: bourbon, rye, and corn. **Bourbon whiskey** is by far the most popular. It is made with at least 51 percent corn, the rest being barley and rye.

Rye whiskey is made with at least 51 percent rye with the balance consisting of corn and barley. **Corn whiskey** is the least produced of the three and contains 80 percent corn and the rest a combination of rye and barley. Only those straight whiskies distilled in Bourbon County, Kentucky, can be labeled "bourbon." Some patrons may expect true bourbon when ordering bourbon without distinguishing a name brand, others simply want bar whiskey. Top bar brands include but are not limited to Jim Beam (bourbon), Wild Turkey (straight), Early Times (blended), Jack Daniel's (blended), and Seagram's 7 (blended).

CANADIAN WHISKY: Whiskies of Canada are blended, usually of the rye variety. These whiskies are usually lighter in body and smoother than American whiskey. Top-call Canadian whiskies include Crown Royal, Canadian Club, Seagram's V.O., and Canadian Mist.

IRISH WHISKEY: Arguably the oldest of all (Ireland's Bushmills distilling house dates back to 1608, making it the oldest distiller in the world), Irish whiskey is a blend of grain whiskies and barley malt whiskies giving it a full barley flavor with a lot of bite. Irish whiskey is popular as a neat shot as well as in the famous Irish Coffee. Top-call Irish whiskies include Bushmills and Jameson.

SCOTCH WHISKY: Simply called "Scotch," whiskies of this origin are legendary for their peaty smoothness and smoky flavor. Their unique flavor is derived in great part from the process by which the malt barley is dried over peat fires. Scotch is made in both the straight and blended varieties, and all blends contain grain and malt whiskies. The top whiskies of Scotland are of the single malt or straight type. This class of whiskey has many ardent fans. This is part due to the fact that Scotch is rarely mixed with anything except water, so its taste is very discernible. The most popular mass-produced call brands of Scotch include Glenlivet (single malt/straight), Glenfiddich (single malt/straight), Johnnie Walker (blended), Chivas Regal (blended), Dewar's White Label (blended), J&B (blended), and Cutty Sark (blended).

LIQUEUR

Liqueurs or cordials, as they are often called, are for the most part sweeter than liquors. They can be divided into several different broad categories though most taste either fruity, nutty, or minty.

Amaretto:
This almond-flavored liqueur is very popular with younger drinkers, especially women. Amaretto is often mixed with sweet and sour mix and/or orange juice. Amaretto di Saronno is the most popular brand-name amaretto.

Anisette:
This liqueur, which tastes like licorice, is seldom ordered, but when ordered is usually requested straight chilled.

Bénédictine*:
This herb-based liqueur is popular among older drinkers. It is usually served straight up, or on the rocks with brandy and called a "B&B." Due to the popularity of the B&B, the Bénédictine company combined the two ingredients in a bottle appropriately named "B&B," which can be found behind most bars.

Cacao, Crème de:
This chocolate-flavored liqueur comes in both dark and white versions.

Campari*:

This bright red liqueur is popular throughout Europe, especially Italy, where it is made, and it is catching on in the States. Campari tastes like quinine (tonic water) and is usually served either on the rocks or mixed with soda water or tonic water.

Cassis, Crème de:

This liqueur is made from black currants, a sweet-tasting berry. It's used in the Sex on the Beach shot/drink, very popular among young adults, as well as in a Kir, where it is combined with white wine.

Chambord*:

This sweet-tasting French liqueur is made primarily from black raspberries, fruit, and honey. It's popularity is growing, especially as an ingredient in specialty shots.

Chartreuse*:

This rich and aromatic herbal liqueur made by Carthusian monks since 1605 comes in two different versions, yellow and green. Over 130 herbs and spices are aged to create this unique looking and tasting liqueur.

Cointreau*:

This is the best-known brand name of triple sec. Though triple sec is present in many drinks as a secondary mixer, Cointreau is seldom "called" in these drinks, though at times ordered straight up.

Curaçao:

This orange-flavored liqueur comes in many colors, but usually blue or orange. It can be used in place of triple sec, or to add color to a drink.

Drambuie*:

Made from Scotch and heather honey, this liqueur is a popular after-dinner drink, and when combined with Scotch makes a Rusty Nail.

Frangelico*:

This hazelnut-flavored liqueur is seldom served but it is used in the Russian Quaalude, a popular drink on the rocks or as a shot.

Galliano*:

This yellow Italian liqueur which comes in the tall thin bottle is sweet and spicy. It is seldom used except for Harvey Wallbangers and the occasional mixed shot.

Grand Marnier*:

The most popular proprietary orange-flavored liqueur. Grand Marnier is not technically a triple sec; it is more closely associated with curaçao, however, it (as any orange-flavored liqueur) can be used instead of triple sec. Grand Marnier is frequently ordered straight up.

Irish Cream:

This sweet tasting and very rich liqueur made from Irish whiskey and cream has recently become very popular. It is often served on the rocks and is enjoyed in many a shot. There are many quality proprietary liqueurs in this class, the most famous of which is Baileys.

Irish Mist*:

This liqueur, similar to Drambuie in that it is made from whiskey, though Irish, and heather honey, is sweet tasting and very popular served as a shot or straight up on St. Patrick's Day.

Jägermeister*:

This mint-flavored liqueur (technically a bitter) is very popular among young adults. It is almost exclusively ordered as a shot, chilled.

Kahlúa*:
This most popular coffee-flavored liqueur from Mexico is most often used in shots, as well as in both White and Black Russians.

Maraschino:
A sweet cherry liqueur, technically a brandy, which is infrequently used, and then, usually in small quantities.

Menthe, Crème de:
This sweet minty liqueur comes in either green or clear, although the taste is the same. Crème de menthe is used in the Grasshopper, the Stinger, and the Irish Coffee, as well as the occasional after-dinner drink. Green crème de menthe has also found its niche as a dessert topping for vanilla ice cream.

Midori*:
This proprietary brand of melon liqueur is green in color and tastes like a combination between watermelon and cantaloupe. It is used in many of the newer mixed drinks and shots.

Noyau, Crème de:
An almond-flavored liqueur which is seldom used except for the occasional mixed drink or shot.

Ouzo:
This national drink of Greece is anise-based (tastes like licorice) and is ordered often as a shot, chilled.

Pernod*:
A proprietary licorice-flavored absinthe liqueur from France.

Sake:
This unique Japanese drink is brewed from fermented rice, though because of its high alcohol content and taste it is usually thought of as a wine or a liqueur. Technically it is a beer. Most bars do not have sake because it is very rarely ordered, but many Japanese restaurants carry it.

Sambuca:
This licorice-flavored Italian liqueur is very popular served as a chilled shot. It is translucent and colorless, but achieves a cloudy appearance when chilled.

Schnapps:
This category of light and flavorful liqueurs is becoming more and more popular in America. Schnapps flavors include the ever-popular peppermint as well as many new flavors such as root beer, cinnamon, cola, peach, butterscotch, and more.

Sloe Gin:
This sweet-tasting, fruity liqueur made from sloe berries is used in the frequently ordered and aptly named Sloe Gin Fizz.

Southern Comfort*:
This peach-flavored American liqueur is popular served as a shot, or in mixed drinks such as the Alabama Slammer.

Tia Maria*:
This coffee-flavored liqueur is made from rum and spices. It is often used in shots, less often as an after-dinner drink on the rocks.

Triple Sec:
This orange-flavored liqueur is a very common

ingredient in mixed drinks. The most popular proprietary brand is Cointreau.

Vermouth:

This spirit, technically a wine, comes in two types, dry and sweet. Unlike most other liqueurs, vermouth will become stale if left unrefrigerated at length after opening. *Dry vermouth* is extremely strong tasting. It is used in the making of Martinis, and due to its strong taste a Dry Martini should only contain a few drops. *Sweet vermouth* is, as its name implies, sweet. It is used in the Manhattan and is at times ordered on the rocks.

Yukon Jack*:

This strong Canadian whisky– based liqueur has citrus and herb flavors and is served as a neat shot or in specialty shots such as the Jackhammer.

*Denotes those liqueurs which are proprietary (brand name), all others are classes of liquor.

BEER

Brewed and fermented cereal grains are the most ancient of all alcoholic beverages, dating back to 7000 B.C. The predominant cereal used in the production of beer is barley, which is roasted then combined with other cereal grains and cooked with water. The liquid residue of this process is called wort, which is then extracted, combined with hops, and boiled in a kettle. The hops are then removed, and yeast is added, as the catalyst in the fermentation process. The yeast consumes the malt sugar, the by-product of which is alcohol. Beer should be stored in a cool, dry place away from any direct light, especially sunlight.

Ale:

This top-fermented brew is growing in popularity. It originated in Britain, and is now being produced with great success by the micro-breweries of North America. Ale is a full-bodied beer with a strong taste of hops. It ranges in color from a deep copper to pale lighter ales, which approach the almost clear appearance of a lager.

Bock:

This class of beer first produced in Germany is a stronger (6 to 13 percent alcohol) and more full-bodied class of lager beer. It is also a seasonal beer produced in both the spring and fall.

Creme Ale:

A combination of ale and lager are blended together to create this highly carbonated beer.

Lager:

This beer is what most people drink when they simply order a "beer" or "light beer." All of the mass-produced American beers are lagers, as are most of the beers produced in the world. Lager is produced via bottom fermentation, the youngest of beer-production processes, which creates a clear-bodied beer with more stability and effervescence; however, to the lovers of the older methods of production, taste and character are lost in beers produced by this method.

Malt Liquor:

This American beer has a great deal of variation in taste and color. The color can range from light to dark, and the flavor can range from very subtle to very hoppy. The alcohol content of malt liquor is higher than that of most beers, generally over 5 percent.

Pilsner:

This bottom-fermented beer is light golden in

color and has a crisp, clean taste. Pilsner derives its name from the Bohemian city of Pilsen where this type of beer was first brewed.

Porter:
This top-fermented ale is very bitter. Porter is full-bodied and rich, very similar to stout in most aspects, though not as strong.

Stout:
This darkest of beers is very creamy and strong. It is most commonly associated with the British Isles where the most well-known stout, Guinness, of Ireland is made.

Weisse Beer:
As with other beers, this type of beer is brewed with barley. However, unique to weisse beer is that a percentage of wheat is also added. If a bar offers weisse beer it should have large pilsner glasses, sometimes referred to as weisse beer glasses because those who drink this type of beer usually request a large slice of lemon to add to the drink.

WINE

Produced from the fermentation of grapes, wine dates back over six thousand years. After harvesting the grape, primarily in the fall when the grape is at its ripest, the fruit is crushed and pressed to remove all stems and skin. The juice is then placed in a vat and allowed to ferment under the influence of natural grape yeast. When this process is complete, the resulting wine is aged in casks. Only after the wine has been sufficiently aged is it ready for bottling.

There are a myriad of different grapes used in the production of wine. Knowing the variety of grape will give the connoisseur a rough idea of the characteristics of that wine. Although one variety of grape may be grown in several different regions of the world, each will contain certain characteristics inherent to that region. The variety of grape is, however, only one factor in the formation of wine. The vineyard soil, climate, and the techniques employed in production can have a greater effect on the wine than even the grape's variety. The final variable in the making of wine is its vintage, or year in which it was produced. Certain climatic and atmospheric conditions as well as mold, rot, and pests can have great impact on the quality of the grape, affecting the wine it will produce.

The varieties of grape number in the thousands. However, there are only a few varieties which, due to their outstanding characteristics, have been selected by winemakers for cultivation in many regions of the world. Most of the varieties have their origins in the vineyards of Europe. Some of the most popular white wines are derived from the following grape varieties: Chablis, Chardonnay, Chenin Blanc, Fumé Blanc, Sauvignon Blanc, and Riesling. Some of the most popular red wines are derived from the following grape varieties: Burgundy, Cabernet Sauvignon, Chianti, Merlot, Pinot Noir, and Zinfandel.

MIXERS

Bitters:

This bitter-tasting mixer, which contains alcohol, has seen a steady decline in its use over the past few decades. Though called for in many drinks, bitters are often omitted. There are many different types of bitters. Angostura bitters are the most popular and are found behind most bars. A few drops of Angostura bitters will give any drink a strong taste. A popular bartender's myth for curing hiccups is a glass of soda water and a dash of bitters.

Club Soda or Soda Water:

This is simply carbonated water. This mixer is located in the soda gun, if the bar is equipped with one.

Cream:

In the past, heavy or whipping cream was used in the making of many drinks. Today regular cream has replaced heavy cream. Cream is lighter than heavy cream and therefore allows the drinker to consume more drinks before feeling full.

Grenadine:

This sweet red syrup made from pomegranates is used in small quantities in many drinks. It is usually contained in a 12-ounce bottle.

Lime Juice:

This mixer is used in small doses in many drinks. Rose's is the most popular brand. It usually comes in a 12-ounce bottle.

Sour Mix:

Also called "sweet and sour mix," it's a combination of lemon juice, lime juice, and sugar. This mixer is used in many drinks including Collinses, Fizzes, Margaritas, and, of course, Sours. Sour mix is either found in large plastic mixing bottles in the bar's speed rack or in the soda gun.

Tonic Water:

This mixer is flavored with lemon, lime, and quinine. Tonic water is almost always found in the soda gun (its button is usually *Q* for quinine).

AMERICA'S MOST POPULAR DRINKS

When giving recipes to mixed drinks, the other guides list the calculated measurement of each ingredient as if each drink were to be made with a measuring cup, a tablespoon, and a teaspoon. This is not how mixing drinks should be done. Bartending is an art, not a science, and for that reason the bartender must learn to use the tools at his or her disposal. A measuring cup and measuring spoons do not fall into this category. In a perfect world, drink recipes given in ounces would be fine, but behind a busy bar this is not possible. This is impossible for two reasons: first, the bar environment rarely leaves the bartender enough time to slowly and carefully measure each ingredient as the other guides would have you do. More importantly, liquor measurements should be given with regard to the shot because this measurement is determined by the given bar and not by the bartending guide. Even in the comfort of your own home, who wants to measure every ingredient precisely before adding it to a drink.

The system which *The Perfect Cocktail* employs is not only based on the shot glass, but also the bar glass. Using the correct bar glass insures that the ingredients including the mixers will be properly regulated. The secondary mixer is usually such a small amount, usually a splash or a dash, it can be estimated by the bartender. Primary mixers are listed without any measurement at all, but you should remember some drinks have more than one primary mixer. If more than one primary mixer is required, add equal parts of each. When pouring primary mixers, fill the glass up leaving a little more than half an inch at the rim. This space is to avert spillage or for the secondary mixers if they have yet to be added to the drink. If a drink has the option of being served straight up, ounces will be given for the drink's ingredients. This is because straight-up drinks are made in a shaker, and so cannot be regulated by the glass in which they are served. If the drink is to be served on the rocks, disregard the ounces in the recipe and simply serve in the appropriate glass. In all drinks other than those which can be ordered "straight up," secondary mixers will be the only part of the recipe given as ounces, a splash, or a dash. A splash is a little less than $\frac{1}{2}$ ounce, a dash is several drops. This system is very easy to learn and allows the bartender to work quickly while keeping his or her mind from being cluttered with measurements that are better regulated by the bar glass.

Next to each recipe is an illustration of the type of glass used. Some of the drinks include two glasses, often a small rocks glass and a cocktail glass. Whenever these two glasses appear with a drink recipe, it means that the given drink can either be served on the rocks or straight up, chilled. If someone orders one of these drinks, you should ask how they want their drink, straight up or on the rocks. The reason for the two glasses is that these drinks were originally intended to be chilled and served straight up in a cocktail glass. Today, the trend is toward serving these drinks on the rocks in a small rocks glass. In most cases, the first glass depicted should be your first choice in which to serve the drink, but either is appropriate. There are other drinks, such as Sours and Margaritas, which have a choice of glasses based on how the drink is to be served. The description of each glass in the chapter entitled "Bar Glasses" will give you a better understanding of when each glass is to be used.

ALABAMA SLAMMER

- ¾ shot amaretto
- ¾ shot Southern Comfort
- Splash of sloe gin
- Orange juice
- Pineapple juice

Stir.

AMARETTO SOUR

- 1 shot amaretto
- Sour mix
- Orange slice

Shake and garnish.

AMARETTO STONE SOUR

- 1 shot amaretto
- Sour mix
- Orange juice
- Orange slice

Shake and garnish.

BAY BREEZE

- 1 shot vodka
- Pineapple juice
- Cranberry juice

Stir.

BLACK RUSSIAN

- 1 shot vodka
- ½ shot coffee-flavored liqueur (Kahlúa)

Stir.

BLOODY MARY

- 1 shot vodka
- Tomato juice

- Splash of lemon juice
- Dash of Worcestershire sauce
- Dash of Tabasco sauce
- Sprinkle of celery salt or pepper
- Celery stalk or lime wedge

Garnish and serve.

BLUE HAWAIIAN
- ½ shot rum
- ½ shot blue curaçao
- ½ shot crème de coconut
- Pineapple juice
- Cherry

Blend with ice and garnish.

BRANDY ALEXANDER
- ½ shot brandy
- ½ shot crème de cacao (dark)
- Splash of cream

Shake.

CAPE CODDER
- 1 shot vodka
- Cranberry juice
- Lime wedge

Stir and garnish.

CUBA LIBRE
- 1 shot rum
- Cola
- Splash of lime juice
- Lime wedge

Garnish and serve.

DAIQUIRI
- 1 shot rum
- Splash of lime juice
- 1 teaspoon/packet sugar

Shake.

FRAPPÉ

- 1 shot any liqueur

Pour liqueur over shaved/crushed ice in a champagne flute or cocktail glass. Serve.

FROZEN DAIQUIRI

- 1 shot rum
- Splash of triple sec
- 1 ounce lime juice
- 1 teaspoon/packet sugar

Blend with ice.

FUZZY NAVEL

- 1 shot peach schnapps
- Orange juice
- Orange slice

Garnish and serve.

GIMLET

- 1 shot gin
- ¾ ounce lime juice
- Lime wedge

Stir.

GIN AND TONIC

- 1 shot gin
- Tonic water
- Lime wedge

Garnish and serve.

GRASSHOPPER

- ½ shot crème de menthe (green)
- ½ shot crème de cacao (white)
- ¾ ounce cream

Shake.

GREYHOUND/SALTY DOG

- 1 shot vodka
- Grapefruit juice

stir. (Salty Dog: Salt rim of glass.)

IRISH COFFEE

- 1 shot Irish whiskey
- Black coffee to within ½ inch of rim
- 1 teaspoon/packet sugar
- Whipped cream, topped with a splash of crème de menthe (green)

Serve.

HARVEY WALLBANGER

- ¾ shot vodka
- Orange juice
- ¼ shot Galliano, floated on top

Serve.

KAMIKAZE

- ¾ shot vodka
- ¾ shot triple sec
- ¾ ounce lime juice

Shake.

KIR

- 3 ounces white wine
- Splash of crème de cassis
- Lemon twist

Pour over ice and garnish. (Lemon twist is optional but most bartenders include it. Do not stir.)

LONG ISLAND ICED TEA

- ½ shot vodka
- ½ shot gin
- ½ shot rum
- ½ shot tequila
- Splash of triple sec
- Sour mix
- Splash of cola
- Lemon slice

Garnish and serve.

LYNCHBURG LEMONADE

- 1 shot Jack Daniel's
- Splash of triple sec
- Sour mix
- Lemon-lime soda
- Lemon slice

Garnish and serve.

MADRAS

- 1 shot vodka
- Orange juice
- Cranberry juice
- Lime wedge

Garnish and serve.

MAI TAI

- ½ shot rum
- ½ shot dark rum
- ¼ shot curaçao
- Splash of grenadine
- Splash of lime juice
- Splash of orgeat (almond syrup)
- Cherry

Shake.

MANHATTAN

- 1 shot blended whiskey
- ½ shot sweet vermouth
- Cherry

Stir and garnish.

PERFECT MANHATTAN

- 1 shot blended whiskey
- Dash of sweet vermouth
- Dash of dry vermouth
- Cherry

Stir and garnish.

Prior to making a Margarita ask the patron two important questions:

1. Would you like the rim salted? If you are unable to ask, salt the rim.

2. Would you like it straight up, on the rocks, or frozen?

A Margarita straight up is served in a cocktail glass.

A Margarita on the rocks is served in either a small rocks glass or a Margarita glass.

A Frozen Margarita is served in a stemmed goblet, either a Margarita glass, Whiskey Sour glass, or large wineglass.

MARGARITA

Salt rim (if desired).

- 1 shot tequila
- ¼ shot triple sec
- Sour mix
- Splash of lime juice
- Lime wedge (on request)

Shake. For Frozen Margarita, blend with ice.

GOLDEN MARGARITA

Salt rim (if desired)

- 1 shot José Cuervo 1800 tequila or other premium gold tequila
- ¼ shot Cointreau
- Sour mix
- Splash of orange juice
- Splash of lime juice
- Lime wedge (on request)

Shake to make the Margarita up or on the rocks. Blend with ice for Frozen Margarita. Garnish.

BLUE MARGARITA
Salt rim (if desired)
- 1 shot tequila
- ¼ shot blue curaçao
- Sour mix
- Splash of lime juice

Shake.

STRAWBERRY MARGARITA
Salt rim (if desired)
- 1 shot tequila
- ½ shot strawberry liqueur
- ¼ shot triple sec
- 1 ounce sour mix
- 3 ounces strawberry mix
- Strawberry or lime wedge

Blend with ice and garnish.

MARTINIS

Prior to making a Martini ask the patron four important questions:

1. Will this be a Gin or Vodka Martini? If for some reason you are unable to ask (waitress forgets, too busy, etc.), assume gin.

2. Would you like it straight up or on the rocks? If for some reason you are unable to ask, assume straight up.

3. Would you like it dry? This is an important question and should be asked, if unable to ask, make it dry, vermouth can always be added.

4. Would you like a garnish? Most prefer a twist of lemon, some an olive.

A Gibson is a Martini, usually dry, garnished with a cocktail onion.

MARTINI

If it's on the rocks, add ice.

- 1½ shots gin
- Dash of dry vermouth
- Desired garnish

Stir and garnish.

If it's straight up, fill shaker with ice, and fill with:

- 1½ shots gin
- Dash of dry vermouth
- Desired garnish

Stir and strain into cocktail glass. Garnish.

DRY MARTINI

If it's on the rocks, add ice.

- 1½ shots gin
- ½ dash of dry vermouth
- Desired garnish

Stir and garnish.

If it's straight up, fill shaker with ice and fill with:

- 1½ shots gin
- ½ dash of dry vermouth
- Desired garnish

Stir and strain into cocktail glass. Garnish.

EXTRA DRY MARTINI

Add splash of dry vermouth to either empty rocks glass or cocktail glass, depending on whether drink is ordered "on the rocks" or "straight up." Swish dry vermouth around in empty glass and dump it out.

If it's on the rocks, add ice to small rocks glass.

- 1½ shots gin
- 1–2 drops of dry vermouth

- Desired garnish

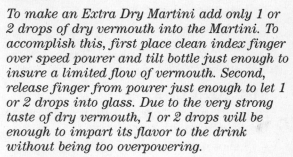

Stir and garnish

Straight up, fill shaker with ice. Fill with:

- 1½ shots gin
- 1 drop of dry vermouth
- Desired garnish

Stir and strain into cocktail glass.
Garnish.

To make an Extra Dry Martini add only 1 or 2 drops of dry vermouth into the Martini. To accomplish this, first place clean index finger over speed pourer and tilt bottle just enough to insure a limited flow of vermouth. Second, release finger from pourer just enough to let 1 or 2 drops into glass. Due to the very strong taste of dry vermouth, 1 or 2 drops will be enough to impart its flavor to the drink without being too overpowering.

MELON BALL

- ½ shot vodka
- ½ shot melon liqueur (Midori)
- Pineapple juice
- Orange slice

Garnish and serve.

OLD-FASHIONED

- 1 shot blended whiskey
- 1 teaspoon/packet sugar
- Dash of bitters
- Dash of water

Stir.

PIÑA COLADA

- 1½ shots rum
- 4 ounces pineapple juice and 2 ounces coconut milk; OR 6 ounces piña colada mix
- Cherry

Blend with ice and garnish.

ROASTED TOASTED ALMOND

- ½ shot amaretto
- ½ shot coffee-flavored liqueur (Kahlúa)
- ½ shot vodka
- Cream

Shake.

ROB ROY

- 1 shot Scotch whisky
- ½ shot sweet vermouth
- Cherry

Stir and garnish.

RUM AND COKE

(A Captain and Coke is a Rum and Coke with Captain Morgan's spiced rum.)

- 1 shot rum
- Cola

Serve.

RUSTY NAIL

- 1 shot Scotch whisky
- ½ shot Drambuie

Stir.

SCREWDRIVER

- 1 shot vodka
- Orange juice

Serve.

SEABREEZE

- 1 shot vodka
- Grapefruit juice
- Cranberry juice
- Lime wedge

Stir and garnish.

7 & 7

- 1 shot Seagram's 7 whiskey
- Lemon-lime soda (7-Up)

Serve.

SEX ON THE BEACH

- ¾ shot crème de cassis
- ¾ shot melon liqueur (Midori)
- Pineapple juice

Serve.

SLOE DRIVER

- 1 shot sloe gin
- Orange juice

Serve.

SLOE GIN FIZZ

- 1 shot sloe gin
- Sour mix
- Splash of soda water
- Cherry

Shake with ice prior to adding soda water.
Garnish.

SLOE SCREW

- ¾ shot vodka
- ¼ shot sloe gin
- Orange juice

Serve.

SPRITZER

- 3 ounces white wine
- Soda water

Serve.

STINGER

- ¾ shot brandy
- ¾ shot crème de menthe (white)

Stir.

STRAWBERRY DAIQUIRI

- 1 shot rum
- ½ shot strawberry liqueur
- 2 ounces strawberry mix or fresh strawberries
- Splash of lime juice

Blend with ice.

TEQUILA SUNRISE

- 1 shot tequila
- Orange juice
- Dash of grenadine

Stir.

TOASTED ALMOND

- ¾ shot amaretto
- ¾ shot coffee-flavored liqueur (Kahlúa)
- Cream

Shake.

TOM COLLINS

- 1 shot gin
- Sour mix
- Splash of soda water
- Cherry and orange slice

Shake with ice prior to adding soda water. Garnish.

VODKA GRASSHOPPER

- ½ shot vodka
- ½ shot crème de menthe (green)
- ½ shot crème de cacao (white)
- Splash of cream

Shake.

VODKA STINGER

- ¾ shot vodka
- ¾ shot crème de menthe (white)

Stir.

VODKA AND TONIC

- 1 shot vodka
- Tonic water
- Lime wedge

Garnish and serve.

WATERMELON

- ½ shot vodka
- ½ shot strawberry liqueur
- Orange juice

Serve.

WHISKEY SOUR

- 1 shot whiskey
- Sour mix
- Cherry and lemon slice

Shake and garnish.

WHITE RUSSIAN

- 1 shot vodka
- ½ shot coffee-flavored liqueur (Kahlúa)
- Cream

Shake.

WOO WOO

- ½ shot vodka
- ½ shot peach schnapps
- Cranberry juice

Stir.

MIXED SHOTS

This section contains the most extensive list of mixed shots to be found in any book. It should be noted that drink recipes, especially shot recipes, vary from region to region. *The Perfect Cocktail* has made every attempt to use the most widely accepted recipe for each shot.

The ingredients of these mixed shots are not presented in ounces, as in other guides, but rather in fractions of a shot. This is done for two reasons: 1) because each individual bar determines the size of its shot; and 2) because mixed shots are from time to time ordered as mixed drinks. The bartender has a great deal of leeway when making mixed drinks that were originally intended as shots. There are no hard-and-fast rules regarding this aspect of bartending, so it's okay to experiment.

Some of these shots when made as a mixed drink are better tasting when more mixer is used and served in a large rocks glass. Others benefit from not having as much mixer and served in a small rocks glass. If ordered as a mixed drink, a shot that is all liquor, with no mixer, should be served as an on-the-rocks drink (a shot and a half) in a small rocks glass.

ALABAMA SLAMMER
- $\frac{1}{5}$ shot amaretto
- $\frac{1}{5}$ shot Southern Comfort

- ⅕ shot sloe gin
- ⅕ shot orange juice
- ⅕ shot pineapple juice

Chill in shaker.

ANTIFREEZE

- ½ shot vodka
- ½ shot crème de menthe (green)

Chill.

B-52

- ⅓ shot coffee-flavored liqueur (Kahlúa)
- ⅓ shot Irish cream
- ⅓ shot Grand Marnier

Layer.

BABE RUTH

- ½ shot hazelnut liqueur (Frangelico)
- ½ shot vodka
- A few peanuts

Layer and garnish.

BALD-HEADED WOMAN

- ¾ shot 151-proof rum
- ¼ shot grapefruit juice

Chill.

BARN BURNER

- ½ shot vodka
- ½ shot tomato juice
- Dash of Tabasco sauce

Pour directly into glass.

BETWEEN THE SHEETS

- ⅓ shot brandy
- ⅓ shot triple sec
- ⅓ shot rum
- Dash of lime juice

Chill.

BIKINI LINE

- ⅓ shot vodka
- ⅓ shot Tia Maria
- ⅓ shot Chambord

Chill.

BLACK ORCHID

- ¼ shot rum
- ¼ shot blue curaçao
- ¼ shot grenadine
- ¼ shot cranberry juice
- Dash of lemon-lime soda

Chill.

BLOODY STOOL

- ¼ shot Irish cream
- ¼ shot 151-proof rum
- ¼ shot Campari
- ¼ shot lime juice

Serve.

BLOW JOB

- ⅗ shot Irish cream
- ⅖ shot vodka
- 1–1½ inches of whipped cream for topping

Pour directly into glass, then top. Drinker should bend over and pick shot glass up with his/her mouth, no hands. Take shot down by bending head back and letting shot pour down throat.

BLUE MARLIN

- ¾ shot rum
- ¼ shot blue curaçao
- Dash of lime juice

Chill.

BOILERMAKER

- 1 shot blended whiskey
- 1 mug of beer

This drink can be drunk in any of a number of ways. 1. Shoot the whiskey straight and drink the beer. 2. Pour the whiskey into the beer and drink the mix. 3. Drop the shot, glass and all, into the beer and chug the mix (also called a Depth Charge).

BRAIN
- ¾ shot Irish cream
- ¼ shot peach schnapps

Serve.

BRAIN HEMORRHAGE
- ¾ shot Irish cream
- ¼ shot peach schnapps
- Dash of grenadine

Serve.

BUBBLE GUM
- ¼ shot vodka
- ¼ shot crème de banana
- ¼ shot peach schnapps
- ¼ shot orange juice

Chill.

BUFFALO SWEAT
- ⅓ shot tequila
- ⅓ shot 151-proof rum
- ⅓ shot Tabasco sauce

Serve.

BUTTERY FINGER
- ¼ shot vodka
- ¼ shot Irish cream
- ¼ shot butterscotch schnapps
- ¼ shot coffee-flavored liqueur (Kahlúa)

Chill.

BUTTERY NIPPLE

- ⅓ shot vodka
- ⅓ shot Irish cream
- ⅓ shot butterscotch schnapps

Chill.

BUZZARD'S BREATH

- ⅓ shot amaretto
- ⅓ shot peppermint schnapps
- ⅓ shot coffee-flavored liqueur (Kahlúa)

Chill.

CEMENT MIXER

- ¾ shot Irish cream
- ¼ shot lime juice

Pour directly into glass. Let stand for 30 seconds and drink will coagulate.

CHOCOLATE-COVERED CHERRY

- ⅓ shot amaretto
- ⅓ shot coffee-flavored liqueur (Kahlúa)
- ⅓ shot crème de cacao (white)
- Drop of grenadine

Chill in shaker, pour, then add a drop of grenadine in center of drink.

COCAINE SHOOTER

- ⅕ shot vodka
- ⅕ shot Chambord
- ⅕ shot Southern Comfort
- ⅕ shot orange juice
- ⅕ shot cranberry juice

Chill.

COMFORTABLE PIRATE

- ¾ shot spiced rum (Captain Morgan's)
- ¼ shot Southern Comfort
- Dash of pineapple juice

Chill.

COOL-AID SHOT

- ¼ shot amaretto
- ¼ shot Southern Comfort
- ¼ shot melon liqueur (Midori)
- ¼ shot cranberry juice

Chill.

CORDLESS SCREWDRIVER

- 1 shot vodka
- 1 teaspoon/packet sugar
- Orange slice

Pour directly into glass. Put sugar half in shot and half on slice of orange, which is placed on rim of shot glass. Drink shot and take a draw on orange.

COSMOS

- 1 shot vodka
- Dash of lime juice

Chill.

COUGH SYRUP

- ½ shot amaretto
- ½ shot Southern Comfort
- Dash of grenadine

Serve.

DIRTY GIRL SCOUT COOKIE

- ⅔ shot Irish cream
- ⅓ shot crème de menthe (green)

Chill.

DR. PIPPER

- ¾ shot amaretto
- ¼ shot 151-proof rum
- 6 ounces beer in separate glass

Chill. Drop shot into beer and drink.

FIREBALL

- 3/4 shot cinnamon schnapps
- 1/4 shot Tabasco sauce

Serve.

FIRE-BREATHING DRAGON

- 1/3 shot tequila
- 1/3 shot Campari
- 1/3 shot 151-proof rum

Serve.

FOURTH OF JULY

- 1/3 shot grenadine
- 1/3 shot vodka
- 1/3 shot blue curaçao

Layer.

FRENCH CONNECTION

- 1/2 shot Grand Marnier
- 1/2 shot cognac

Serve.

FROG LICK

- 2/5 shot vodka
- 2/5 shot Yukon Jack
- 1/5 shot lime juice

Chill.

FUCK ME UP

- 1/4 shot cinnamon schnapps
- 1/4 shot peppermint schnapps
- 1/4 shot Jägermeister
- 1/4 shot 151-proof rum

Chill prior to adding rum. Float rum on top.

GRAPE CRUSH

- ½ shot vodka
- ½ shot Chambord
- Dash of sour mix

Serve.

GREEN DEMON

- ¼ shot vodka
- ¼ shot rum
- ¼ shot melon liqueur (Midori)
- ¼ shot sour mix

Chill.

GREEN LIZARD

- ¾ shot Chartreuse (green)
- ¼ shot 151-proof rum

Chill.

HAPPY RANCHER SHOT

- ⅕ shot Scotch whisky
- ⅕ shot peach schnapps
- ⅕ shot melon liqueur (Midori)
- ⅕ shot vodka
- ⅕ shot lemon-lime soda

Chill.

HEAD BANGER

- ½ shot ouzo
- ½ shot 151-proof rum
- Dash of grenadine

Chill.

HONOLULU PUNCH SHOT

- ⅕ shot Southern Comfort
- ⅕ shot 151-proof rum
- ⅕ shot amaretto
- ⅕ shot pineapple juice

- ⅕ shot orange juice
- Dash of grenadine

Chill.

HUMMER

- ½ shot rum
- ¼ shot coffee-flavored liqueur (Kahlúa)
- ¼ shot cream

Serve.

HURRICANE

- ½ shot Jägermeister
- ½ shot Yukon Jack
- Dash of Irish cream

Pour directly into glass, drink will swirl like its namesake.

ILLUSION

- ⅕ shot rum
- ⅕ shot vodka
- ⅕ shot triple sec
- ⅕ shot tequila
- ⅕ shot melon liquor (Midori)
- Dash of lime juice

Chill.

INTERNATIONAL INCIDENT

- ⅕ shot amaretto
- ⅕ shot vodka
- ⅕ shot coffee-flavored liqueur (Kahlúa)
- ⅕ shot hazelnut liqueur (Frangelico)
- ⅕ shot Irish cream

Chill.

IRISH CHARLIE

- ½ shot Irish cream
- ½ shot crème de menthe (white)

Chill.

IRISH FLAG

- ⅓ shot crème de menthe (green)
- ⅓ shot Irish cream
- ⅓ shot Grand Marnier

Layer.

JACKHAMMER

- ¾ shot root beer schnapps
- ¼ shot Yukon Jack

Chill.

JÄGER SHAKE

- ⅕ shot Jägermeister
- ⅕ shot Irish cream
- ⅕ shot root beer schnapps
- ⅕ shot amaretto
- ⅕ shot cola

Chill.

JAWBREAKER

- 1 shot cinnamon schnapps
- Dash of Tabasco

Serve.

GELATIN SHOTS

- 6 ounces desired flavor gelatin mix
- 12 ounces vodka
- 12 ounces boiling water

Mix all ingredients in a pan until gelatin has dissolved. Place in refrigerator. Gelatin Shots can be eaten in the jelled form (like gelatin is traditionally eaten), or drunk like a shot. To drink like a shot, remove the mix from the refrigerator before it has jelled.

JELLY BEAN

- ½ shot anisette
- ½ shot blackberry brandy

Chill.

JELLYFISH

- ¼ shot crème de cacao (white)
- ¼ shot amaretto
- ¼ shot Irish cream
- ¼ shot grenadine

Pour first 3 ingredients directly into glass. Pour grenadine in center of glass.

KAMIKAZE

- ⅓ shot vodka
- ⅓ shot triple sec
- ⅓ shot lime juice

Chill.

LEMON DROP

- 1 shot vodka
- 1 teaspoon/packet sugar
- Lemon slice

Pour vodka directly into glass. Then half the sugar in shot and half on slice of lemon, which is placed on rim of shot glass. Drink shot and take a draw on lemon.

LETHAL INJECTION

- ⅙ shot spiced rum (Captain Morgan's)
- ⅙ shot Malibu rum
- ⅙ shot crème de noyau
- ⅙ shot rum
- ⅙ shot orange juice
- ⅙ shot pineapple juice

Chill.

LIMP MOOSE

- ½ shot Canadian whisky
- ½ shot Irish cream

Chill.

LION TAMER
- ¾ shot Southern Comfort
- ¼ shot lime juice

Chill.

LIQUID COCAINE
- ⅖ shot peppermint schnapps
- ⅖ shot Jägermeister
- ⅕ shot 151-proof rum

Chill.

LOBOTOMY
- ⅓ shot amaretto
- ⅓ shot Chambord
- ⅓ shot pineapple juice

Chill.

LUNCH PAIL
- ½ shot amaretto
- ½ shot orange juice
- 6 ounces beer in separate glass

Chill.

MELON BALL
- ⅓ shot melon liqueur (Midori)
- ⅓ shot vodka
- ⅓ shot pineapple juice

Chill.

MIND ERASER
Add ice to small rocks glass.
- ⅓ shot coffee-flavored liqueur (Kahlúa)
- ⅓ shot vodka
- ⅓ shot Jack Daniel's
- Splash of soda water
- Large drinking straw

Suck drink down through straw in one gulp.

NUTTY IRISHMAN

- ½ shot Irish cream
- ½ shot hazelnut liqueur (Frangelico)

Chill.

NUTTY PROFESSOR

- ⅓ shot Irish cream
- ⅓ shot hazelnut liqueur (Frangelico)
- ⅓ shot Grand Marnier

Chill.

ORANGE CRUSH

- ½ shot vodka
- ½ shot triple sec
- Dash of soda water

Serve.

ORGASM

- ⅓ shot amaretto
- ⅓ shot coffee-flavored liqueur (Kahlúa)
- ⅓ shot Irish cream

Chill.

ORIENTAL RUG

- ¼ shot Irish cream
- ¼ shot hazelnut liqueur (Frangelico)
- ¼ shot Jägermeister
- ¼ shot coffee-flavored liqueur (Kahlúa)
- Dash of cola

Chill.

PEACH TART

- ¾ shot peach schnapps
- ¼ shot lime juice

Chill.

PEANUT BUTTER AND JELLY

- ½ shot hazelnut liqueur (Frangelico)
- ½ shot Chambord

Serve.

PIGSKIN

- ⅓ shot vodka
- ⅓ shot melon liqueur (Midori)
- ⅓ shot sour mix

Chill.

PINEAPPLE BOMBER

- ⅓ shot Jack Daniel's
- ⅓ shot Southern Comfort
- ⅓ shot pineapple juice

Chill.

PLENTY & GOOD SHOT

- ½ shot ouzo
- ½ shot coffee-flavored liqueur (Kahlúa)

Chill.

POPPERS

- ¾ shot desired liquor
- Splash of lemon-lime soda

Pour desired liquor directly into glass. Place napkin over the top of the shot glass, take the shot glass in the palm of your hand, and slam shot glass down against top of bar or table and immediately drink. This action will cause the lemon-lime soda to fizz, which will mask the taste of the liquor.

PRAIRIE FIRE

- 1 shot tequila
- Dash of Tabasco sauce

Serve.

PURPLE HAZE

Add ice to small rocks glass.

- $2/5$ shot vodka
- $2/5$ shot Chambord
- $1/5$ shot triple sec
- Splash of lime juice
- Splash of soda water
- Large drinking straw

Suck drink down through straw in one gulp.

PURPLE HOOTER

- $1/4$ shot Chambord
- $1/4$ shot vodka
- $1/4$ shot sour mix
- $1/4$ shot lemon-lime soda

Chill.

RED DEATH

- $1/5$ shot amaretto
- $1/5$ shot sloe gin
- $1/5$ shot Southern Comfort
- $1/5$ shot vodka
- $1/5$ shot triple sec
- Dash of orange juice
- Dash of grenadine

Chill.

RED DRAGON

- $1/2$ shot tequila
- $1/2$ shot Campari

Chill.

ROAD KILL

- $1/3$ shot Irish whiskey
- $1/3$ shot Wild Turkey whiskey
- $1/3$ shot 151-proof rum

Chill.

ROCKY MOUNTAIN

- ½ shot amaretto
- ½ shot Southern Comfort
- Dash of lime juice

Chill.

ROOT BEER

- ¼ shot Galliano
- ¼ shot coffee-flavored liqueur (Kahlúa)
- ¼ shot vodka
- ¼ shot cola

Chill.

RUSSIAN QUAALUDE

- ⅕ shot Stolichnaya (or other Russian vodka)
- ⅖ shot hazelnut liqueur (Frangelico)
- ⅖ shot amaretto

Chill.

SAMBUCA SLIDE

- ½ shot sambuca
- ¼ shot vodka
- ¼ shot cream

Chill.

SCOOTER

- ½ shot amaretto
- ½ shot brandy
- Dash of cream

Chill.

SCREAMING ORGASM

- ¼ shot vodka
- ¼ shot coffee-flavored liqueur (Kahlúa)
- ¼ shot Irish cream
- ¼ shot amaretto

Chill.

SEX ON THE BEACH

- ²⁄₅ shot crème de cassis
- ²⁄₅ shot melon liqueur (Midori)
- ¹⁄₅ shot pineapple juice

Chill.

SILK PANTIES

- ½ shot vodka
- ½ shot peach schnapps

Chill.

SILVER SPIDER

- ¼ shot vodka
- ¼ shot rum
- ¼ shot triple sec
- ¼ shot crème de menthe (white)

Chill.

SLIPPERY DICK

- ²⁄₅ shot crème de banana
- ³⁄₅ shot Irish cream

Chill.

SLIPPERY NIPPLE

- ²⁄₅ shot peppermint schnapps
- ²⁄₅ shot Irish cream
- ¹⁄₅ shot grenadine

Serve.

SNAKEBITE

- 1 shot Yukon Jack
- Dash of lime juice

Serve.

SNOWSHOE

- ³⁄₅ shot Wild Turkey whiskey
- ²⁄₅ shot peppermint schnapps

Chill.

S.O.B.

- ⅓ shot brandy
- ⅓ shot Cointreau
- ⅓ shot 151-proof rum

Serve.

STARS AND STRIPES

- ⅓ shot grenadine
- ⅓ shot cream
- ⅓ shot blue curaçao

Layer.

STORM TROOPER

- ½ shot Jägermeister
- ½ shot peppermint schnapps

Chill.

STRAWBERRY SHORTCAKE SHOT

- ⅖ shot strawberry liqueur
- ⅖ shot vodka
- ⅕ shot cream

Chill.

SWEET TART SHOT

- ⅖ shot melon liqueur (Midori)
- ⅖ shot Southern Comfort
- ⅕ shot sour mix

Chill.

TEQUILA SHOT

- 1 shot tequila
- Pinch of salt
- Lime wedge

Lick the salt, drink the shot, suck the lime.

TERMINATOR

- ⅕ shot coffee-flavored liqueur (Kahlúa)
- ⅕ shot Irish cream
- ⅕ shot sambuca

- ⅕ shot Grand Marnier
- ⅕ shot vodka

Layer.

THREE WISE MEN
- ⅓ shot Jack Daniel's
- ⅓ shot Jim Beam
- ⅓ shot Johnnie Walker Red

Serve.

TOOTSIE SHOT
- ½ shot coffee-flavored liqueur (Kahlúa)
- ½ shot orange juice

Chill.

TO THE MOON
- ¼ shot amaretto
- ¼ shot Irish cream
- ¼ shot coffee-flavored liqueur (Kahlúa)
- ¼ shot 151-proof rum

Chill.

TRIPLE T
- ⅓ shot Tanqueray gin
- ⅓ shot tequila
- ⅓ shot Wild Turkey whiskey

Chill.

VAMPIRE
- ⅓ shot vodka
- ⅓ shot Chambord
- ⅓ shot cranberry juice

Chill.

VULCAN MIND PROBE

- ⅓ shot Irish cream
- ⅓ shot peppermint schnapps
- ⅓ shot 151-proof rum
- Large drinking straw

Layer. Suck drink down through straw in one gulp.

WATERMELON

- ⅓ shot vodka
- ⅓ shot strawberry liqueur
- ⅓ shot orange juice

Chill.

WHITE CLOUDS

- ¾ shot sambuca
- ¼ shot soda water

To achieve cloudy look, sambuca must be chilled.

WINDEX

- ½ shot vodka
- ½ shot blue curaçao

Serve.

WOO WOO

- ⅓ shot vodka
- ⅓ shot peach schnapps
- ⅓ shot cranberry juice

Chill.

YOUR SHOTS AND NOTES

MORE FUN MIXED DRINKS

AMARETTO AND CREAM

- 1 shot amaretto
- 1½ ounces cream

Shake.

AMARETTO ROSE

- 1 shot amaretto
- Splash of Rose's lime juice
- Soda water

Serve.

ANGEL'S DELIGHT

- ¼ shot grenadine
- ¼ shot triple sec
- ¼ shot sloe gin
- ¼ shot cream

Layer.

ANGEL'S KISS

- ¼ shot crème de cacao (white)
- ¼ shot sloe gin
- ¼ shot brandy
- ¼ shot cream

Layer.

APPLE PIE

- 1½ shots apple schnapps
- Splash of cinnamon schnapps
- Sprinkle of ground cinnamon
- Apple slice

Serve.

B&B

- ½ shot Bénédictine
- ½ shot brandy

Layer.

BACARDI

- 1 shot Bacardi rum
- Splash of lime juice
- Splash of grenadine

Shake.

BANANA BALM

- 1 shot vodka
- ¼ shot crème de banana
- Dash of lime juice
- Soda water

Shake first 3 ingredients, then add soda water.

BANSHEE

- ¾ shot crème de banana
- ¾ shot crème de cacao (white)
- Splash of cream

Shake.

BARBARY COAST

- ½ shot gin
- ½ shot rum
- ½ shot Scotch whisky
- ½ shot crème de cacao (white)
- Splash of cream

Shake.

BEACHCOMBER

- ³/₄ shot rum
- ¹/₄ shot triple sec
- Splash of lime juice
- Cherry

Moisten rim of glass with lime and dip in sugar. Shake and garnish.

BELMONT STAKES

- ½ shot vodka
- ¼ shot rum
- ¼ shot strawberry liqueur
- Splash of lime juice
- Dash of grenadine
- Orange slice

Shake. For frozen drink, blend with ice. Garnish.

BLACK AND TAN
(HALF AND HALF)

Equal parts of each.

- Ale
- Stout or porter

Layer over ale using inverted spoon as explained in section on "Layering." This drink is usually comprised of Guinness (black) and Harp (tan).

BLACK HAWK

- ³/₄ shot blended whiskey
- ³/₄ shot sloe gin
- Cherry

Stir and garnish.

BLACK MAGIC

- 1 shot vodka
- ½ shot coffee-flavored liqueur (Kahlúa)
- Dash of lemon juice
- Twist of lemon

Garnish and serve.

BLOODY MARIA

- 1 shot tequila
- Tomato juice
- Splash of lemon juice
- Dash of Worcestershire sauce
- Dash of Tabasco sauce
- Sprinkle of Celery salt or pepper
- Celery stalk or lime wedge

Garnish and serve.

BLUE LAGOON

- ½ shot vodka
- ½ shot blue curaçao
- Lemonade
- Cherry

Garnish and serve.

BLUE MOON

- 1 shot gin
- ½ shot blue curaçao
- Lemon twist

Shake and garnish.

BLUE SHARK

- ¾ shot vodka
- ¾ shot tequila
- Splash of blue curaçao

Shake.

BOBBY BURNS

- ½ shot Scotch whisky
- ½ shot sweet vermouth
- Dash of Bénédictine
- Twist of lemon

Stir and garnish.

BOCCIE BALL

- 1 shot amaretto
- Orange juice
- Soda water
- Orange slice

Garnish and serve.

BOSTON GOLD

- 1 shot vodka
- Splash of crème de banana
- Orange juice

Stir.

BRANDY COLLINS

- 1 shot brandy
- Sour mix
- Splash of soda water
- Cherry and orange slice

Shake brandy and sour mix, then add soda water. Garnish.

BULLFROG

- 1 shot vodka
- Lemonade
- Lime wedge

Garnish and serve.

CAPRI

- ¾ shot crème de cacao (white)
- ¾ shot crème de banana
- Splash of cream

Shake.

CARA SPOSA

- ¾ shot coffee-flavored brandy
- ¾ shot triple sec
- Splash of cream

Shake.

CARIBBEAN CHAMPAGNE

- 6 ounces champagne (chilled)
- Splash of rum
- Splash of crème de banana

Serve.

CARROL COCKTAIL

- 1 shot brandy
- ½ shot sweet vermouth
- Cherry

Stir and garnish.

CASABLANCA

- 1 shot rum
- Dash of triple sec
- Dash of cherry liqueur (Maraschino)
- Dash of lime juice

Shake.

CHAPEL HILL

- 1 shot bourbon whiskey
- ½ shot triple sec
- Dash of lemon juice
- Orange twist

Shake and garnish.

CHERRY BOMB

- ½ shot vodka
- ½ shot rum
- ½ shot tequila
- Pineapple juice
- Coconut milk
- Splash of milk
- Dash of grenadine

Shake.

CHERRY COLA

- 1 shot dark rum
- ½ shot cherry brandy
- Cola

Serve.

CHIQUITA COCKTAIL

- ¾ shot crème de banana
- ¾ shot Cointreau
- Splash of cream

Shake.

CHOCOLATE RUM

- 1 shot rum
- Dash of 151-proof rum
- Dash of crème de cacao (white)
- Dash of crème de menthe (white)
- Dash of cream

Shake.

CLIMAX

- ¼ shot crème de cacao (white)
- ¼ shot amaretto
- ¼ shot triple sec
- ¼ shot vodka
- ¼ shot crème de banana
- 1 ounce cream

Shake.

CREAMSICLE

- 1 shot amaretto
- Orange juice
- Milk or cream

Shake.

CREAM SODA

- 1 shot amaretto
- Soda water

Serve.

CRICKET

- ¾ shot crème de cacao (white)
- ¾ shot crème de menthe (green)
- Dash of brandy
- 1 ounce cream

Shake.

CRUISE CONTROL

- ½ shot rum
- ¼ shot apricot brandy
- ¼ shot Cointreau
- Splash of lemon juice
- Soda water

Shake.

DAMN-THE-WEATHER

- 1 shot gin
- ½ shot sweet vermouth
- Splash of triple sec
- Splash of orange juice

Shake.

DIRTY MOTHER

- 1 shot brandy
- ½ shot coffee-flavored liqueur (Kahlúa)

Stir.

DREAM

- 1 shot brandy
- ½ shot triple sec
- Dash of anisette

Shake.

EGGNOG FOR ONE

- 1 egg
- 1 teaspoon/packet sugar
- 1 shot desired liquor: brandy, rum, whiskey, or a combination
- 6 ounces milk

- Dusting of grated nutmeg

Beat egg and sugar, then shake entire mix with ice and pour into empty highball glass (no ice).

ELECTRIC LEMONADE

- ¼ shot vodka
- ¼ shot gin
- ¼ shot rum
- ¼ shot tequila
- Splash of triple sec
- Sour mix
- Lemon-lime soda

Shake first 6 ingredients with ice, then add lemon-lime soda.

EL SALVADOR COCKTAIL

- 1 shot rum
- ½ shot hazelnut liqueur (Frangelico)
- Splash of lime juice
- Dash of grenadine

Shake.

FIFTY-FIFTY

- ¾ shot gin
- ¾ shot dry vermouth

Stir.

FLYING DUTCHMAN

- 1½ shots gin
- Dash of triple sec

Shake.

FOXY LADY

- ¾ shot amaretto
- ¾ shot crème de cacao (dark)
- 1½ ounces cream

Shake.

FREE SILVER

- ¾ shot gin
- ¼ shot dark rum
- Dash of cream
- Sour mix
- Soda water

Shake first 4 ingredients, then add soda water.

FROSTBITE

- 1 shot tequila
- ¼ shot crème de cacao (white)
- Splash of blue curaçao
- 2 ounces cream

Shake. For frozen drink, blend with ice.

GENOA COCKTAIL

- 1 shot vodka
- ½ shot Campari
- Orange juice

Shake.

GIN CASSIS

- 1 shot gin
- ¼ shot crème de cassis
- Splash of lemon juice

Shake.

GIN FIZZ

- 1 shot gin
- Sour mix
- Splash of soda water

Shake gin and sour mix with ice, then add soda water.

GIN RICKEY

- 1 shot gin
- Soda water
- Splash of lime juice

Stir.

GLOOM CHASER

- ¾ shot Grand Marnier
- ¾ shot curaçao
- Splash of lemon juice
- Dash of grenadine

Shake.

GODCHILD

- ½ shot vodka
- ½ shot amaretto
- Splash of cream

Shake and strain into champagne glass.

GODFATHER

- 1 shot Scotch whisky
- ½ shot amaretto

Stir.

GODMOTHER

- 1 shot vodka
- ½ shot coffee-flavored liqueur (Kahlúa)

Stir.

GOLDEN DREAM

- 1 shot Galliano
- ¼ shot triple sec
- Splash of orange juice
- Splash of cream

Shake.

GORILLA PUNCH

- ¾ shot vodka
- ¼ shot blue curaçao
- Orange juice
- Pineapple juice
- Cherry

Shake and garnish.

GRAND HOTEL

- ¾ shot Grand Marnier
- ¾ shot gin
- Splash of dry vermouth
- Dash of lemon juice
- Lemon twist

Shake and garnish.

GRAND OCCASION COCKTAIL

- 1 shot rum
- ¼ shot Grand Marnier
- ¼ shot crème de cacao (white)
- Dash of lemon juice

Shake.

GREENBACK

- 1 shot gin
- ½ shot crème de menthe (green)
- 1 ounce lemon juice

Shake.

GREEN CHARTREUSE NECTAR

- ¾ shot apricot schnapps
- ½ shot Chartreuse (green)

Serve.

GREEN DRAGON

- 1 shot Stolichnaya (Russian vodka)
- ½ shot Chartreuse (green)

Shake.

GROUND ZERO

- ½ shot bourbon whiskey
- ½ shot peppermint schnapps
- ½ shot vodka
- ¼ shot coffee-flavored liqueur (Kahlúa)

Shake.

HAIRY NAVEL

- ½ shot peach schnapps
- ½ shot vodka
- Orange juice

Serve.

HALLEY'S COMFORT

- ½ shot peach schnapps
- ½ shot Southern Comfort
- Soda water

Serve.

HAMMERHEAD

- ½ shot amaretto
- ½ shot curaçao
- ½ shot rum
- Dash of Southern Comfort

Shake.

HAWAII SEVEN-O

- 1 shot blended whiskey
- ½ shot amaretto
- Orange juice
- Splash of piña colada mix

Shake. For frozen drink, blend with ice.

HIGH ROLLER

- 1 shot vodka
- ½ shot Grand Marnier
- Orange juice
- Dash of grenadine

Shake.

The Perfect Cocktail

HOMECOMING
- ¾ shot amaretto
- ¾ shot Irish cream

Shake.

HOP TOAD
- ½ shot apricot brandy
- ½ shot rum
- Splash of lime juice

Stir.

ICE PICK
- 1 shot vodka
- Iced tea
- Lemon slice

Garnish and serve.

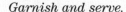

IGUANA
- ½ shot vodka
- ½ shot tequila
- Dash of coffee-flavored liqueur (Kahlúa)
- 2 ounces sour mix

Shake.

INCIDER
- 1 shot blended whiskey
- Apple cider

Serve.

IRISH RICKEY
- 1 shot Irish whiskey
- Soda water
- Splash of lime juice

Stir.

IRISH SHILLELAGH
- 1 shot Irish whiskey
- Splash of sloe gin

- Splash of rum
- Sour mix
- Raspberries, strawberries, peaches, and a cherry

Shake and garnish.

IXTAPA

- 1 shot coffee-flavored liqueur (Kahlúa)
- ½ shot tequila

Stir.

JADE

- 1 shot rum
- Dash of crème de menthe (green)
- Dash of triple sec
- Dash of lime juice
- 1 teaspoon/packet sugar

Shake.

JAMAICAN CREAM

- ¾ shot Myers's dark rum
- ¾ shot triple sec
- Cream

Serve.

JAMAICAN WIND

- 1 shot Myers's dark rum
- ½ shot coffee-flavored liqueur (Kahlúa)
- Cream

Serve.

JOHN COLLINS

- 1 shot blended whiskey
- Sour mix
- Splash of soda water
- Cherry and orange slice

Shake whiskey and sour mix with ice, then add soda water. Garnish.

JUNGLE JIM

- ³/₄ shot vodka
- ³/₄ shot crème de banana
- 1 ounce cream or milk

Shake.

KAHLÚA AND CREAM

- 1½ shots coffee-flavored liqueur (Kahlúa)
- Cream

Stir.

KENTUCKY COCKTAIL

- 1½ shots bourbon whiskey
- 1 ounce pineapple juice

Shake.

KENTUCKY ORANGE BLOSSOM

- 1 shot bourbon whiskey
- Splash of triple sec
- Orange juice

Serve.

KIR ROYALE

- 6 ounces champagne (chilled)
- Splash of crème de cassis

Serve.

KNOCKOUT

- ½ shot apricot brandy
- ½ shot sloe gin
- ½ shot Southern Comfort
- Orange juice

Stir.

KONA COOLER

- 1 shot blended whiskey
- ¼ shot curaçao
- Splash of sweet vermouth
- Splash of lime juice

Serve.

LEPRECHAUN

- 1½ shots Irish whiskey
- Tonic water

Serve.

LIMBO

- 1 shot rum
- ½ shot crème de banana
- 1 ounce orange juice

Shake.

LIME RICKEY

- 1 shot gin
- Splash of lime juice
- Soda water
- Lime wedge

Garnish and serve.

LONG BEACH ICED TEA

- ¼ shot vodka
- ¼ shot gin
- ¼ shot rum
- ¼ shot tequila
- Splash of triple sec
- Sour mix
- Cranberry juice
- Lemon slice

Garnish and serve.

MALIBU WAVE

- ¾ shot tequila
- ¼ shot triple sec
- Dash of blue curaçao
- 1½ ounces sour mix

Shake.

MAMIE GILROY

- 1 shot Scotch whisky
- Ginger ale
- Splash of lime juice

Serve.

MANDEVILLE

- 1 shot rum
- ½ shot dark rum
- Dash of anisette
- Dash of lemon juice
- Dash of grenadine
- Dash of cola

Shake first 5 ingredients, then add cola.

MARMALADE

- 1 shot curaçao
- Tonic water
- Orange slice

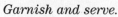

Garnish and serve.

MATADOR

- 1 shot tequila
- 2 ounces pineapple juice
- Splash of lime juice

Shake.

MELON BALL SUNRISE

- ¾ shot vodka
- ¼ shot melon liqueur (Midori)
- Orange juice
- Dash of grenadine

Serve.

MIDNIGHT SUN

- 1½ shots vodka
- Splash of grenadine

Stir.

MIMOSA

- 3 ounces champagne (chilled)
- 3 ounces orange juice

Serve.

MINT JULEP

The Mint Julep is the traditional drink of the Kentucky Derby.

- 4 muddled (crushed) mint leaves
- 2 shots bourbon whiskey
- Dash of water
- 1 teaspoon/packet sugar
- Mint sprig

Stir and garnish.

MOCHA MINT

- ¾ shot coffee-flavored liqueur (Kahlúa)
- ¾ shot crème de cacao (white)
- ¾ shot crème de menthe (white)

Shake.

MONKEY WRENCH

- 1 shot rum
- Grapefruit juice

Stir.

MOSCOW MULE

- 1 shot vodka
- ¾ ounce lime juice
- Ginger ale

Serve.

MOULIN ROUGE

- 1 shot sloe gin
- ½ shot sweet vermouth
- Dash of bitters

Stir.

MUDSLIDE

- ¾ shot vodka
- ¾ shot coffee-flavored liqueur (Kahlúa)
- ¾ shot Irish cream

Shake.

NEGRONI

Ask patron whether drink to be made with sweet or dry vermouth.

- ¾ shot gin
- ¾ shot Campari
- ¾ ounce vermouth (sweet or dry)
- Splash of soda water

Stir.

NINJA TURTLE

- 1 shot gin
- ½ shot blue curaçao
- Orange juice

Stir.

NOCTURNAL

- 1 shot bourbon whiskey
- ½ shot crème de cacao (dark)
- Splash of cream

Shake.

NUTTY STINGER

- 1 shot amaretto
- ½ shot crème de menthe (white)

Shake.

OLYMPIC

- ½ shot brandy
- ½ shot curaçao
- ¾ ounce orange juice

Shake.

ORANGE BLOSSOM

- 1 shot gin
- Orange juice

Serve.

PADDY COCKTAIL

- 1 shot Irish whiskey
- ¾ shot sweet vermouth
- Dash of bitters

Stir.

PAISLEY MARTINI

- 1 shot gin
- Dash of dry vermouth
- Dash of Scotch whisky
- Lemon twist

Stir and garnish.

PANAMA

- ¾ shot dark rum
- ¼ shot crème de cacao (white)
- Cream

Shake.

PAVAROTTI

- 1 shot amaretto
- ¼ shot brandy
- ¼ shot crème de cacao (white)

Shake.

PEPPERMINT PATTY

- ¾ shot crème de cacao (dark)
- ¾ shot crème de menthe (white)
- Cream

Stir.

PERFECT ROB ROY

- 1 shot Scotch whisky
- Dash of sweet vermouth
- Dash of dry vermouth
- Cherry

Stir and garnish.

PINK CREOLE

- 1 shot rum
- Splash of lime juice
- Dash of grenadine
- Dash of cream
- Cherry

Shake and garnish.

PINK LADY

- 1 shot gin
- Splash of grenadine
- 1½ ounces cream

Shake.

PINK LEMONADE

- 1 shot vodka
- Sour mix
- Splash of cranberry juice
- Lemon-lime soda

- Lemon slice

Shake first 3 ingredients, add lemon-lime soda, then garnish.

PINK SQUIRREL

- ½ shot crème de cacao (white)
- ½ shot crème de noyau
- 1 ounce cream

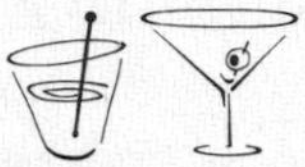

Shake.

PLANTER'S PUNCH

- ¾ shot Myers's dark rum
- ¾ shot rum
- Splash of lime juice
- 1 teaspoon/packet sugar
- Dash of grenadine
- Soda water
- Cherry and orange slice

Shake first 5 ingredients, then add soda water. Garnish.

POPSICLE

- 1 shot amaretto
- Orange juice
- Cream

Stir.

POUSSE-CAFÉ

- ⅕ shot grenadine
- ⅕ shot Chartreuse (yellow)
- ⅕ shot crème de cassis
- ⅕ shot crème de menthe (white)
- ⅕ shot Chartreuse (green)

Layer.

PRESBYTERIAN

- 1 shot whiskey
- Ginger ale
- Soda water

Serve.

PURPLE PASSION

- 1 shot vodka
- Grapefruit juice
- Grape juice

Serve.

QUICKY

- ¾ shot bourbon whiskey
- ¾ shot rum
- Dash of triple sec

Stir.

RAMOS FIZZ

- 1 shot gin
- 1½ ounces sour mix
- Splash of orange juice
- Splash of cream
- 1 egg white
- Soda water

Shake first 5 ingredients, then add soda water.

RASPBERRY SMASH

- ¾ shot vodka
- ¼ shot Chambord
- Pineapple juice

Shake.

RECEPTACLE

- 1 shot vodka
- Splash of cranberry juice
- Splash of orange juice
- Splash of pineapple juice
- Lemon-lime soda
- Cherry and orange slices

Garnish and serve.

RED DEVIL

- ¼ shot vodka
- ¼ shot sloe gin
- ¼ shot Southern Comfort
- ¼ shot triple sec
- ¼ shot crème de banana
- Orange juice
- Dash of lime juice

Shake.

RED LION

- ¾ shot gin
- ¾ shot Grand Marnier
- Splash of orange juice
- Splash of lemon juice

Shake.

RED RUSSIAN

- ¾ shot strawberry liqueur
- ¾ shot vodka
- Cream

Shake.

RICKEY

- 1 shot desired liquor
- Soda water
- Lime wedge.

Garnish and serve.

RITZ FIZZ

- 6 ounces champagne (chilled)
- Dash of amaretto
- Dash of blue curaçao
- Dash of lemon juice
- Lemon twist

Stir and garnish.

ROMAN STINGER

- 1 shot brandy
- ½ shot sambuca
- ½ shot crème de menthe (white)

Shake.

ROSE HALL

- 1 shot dark rum
- ½ shot crème de banana
- 1 ounce orange juice
- Dash of lime juice
- Lime wedge

Shake and garnish.

ROYAL GIN FIZZ

- 1 shot gin
- ½ shot Grand Marnier
- 1 egg white
- Sour mix
- Soda water

Shake first 4 ingredients, then add soda water.

ROYAL SCREW

- 1 shot cognac (brandy)
- 2 ounces orange juice
- Champagne (chilled)

Stir.

RUM RUNNER

- 1 shot gin
- Pineapple juice
- Splash of lime juice
- 1 teaspoon/packet sugar
- Dash of bitters

Shake.

RUPTURED DUCK

- ¾ shot crème de banana
- ¾ shot crème de noyau
- 1 ounce cream

Shake.

RUSSIAN

- ¾ shot gin
- ¾ shot vodka
- ¾ shot crème de cacao (white)

Shake.

RUSSIAN BANANA

- ½ shot vodka
- ½ shot crème de banana
- ½ shot crème de cacao (dark)
- 1 ounce cream

Shake.

ST. PAT'S

- ½ shot crème de menthe (green)
- ½ shot Chartreuse (green)
- ½ shot Irish whiskey

Serve.

SAVE THE PLANET

- ¾ shot melon liqueur (Midori)
- ¾ shot vodka
- Splash of blue curaçao
- Dash of Chartreuse (green)

Shake.

SAXON

- 1½ shots rum
- Splash of lime juice
- Dash of grenadine
- Orange twist

Shake and garnish.

SCARLETT O'HARA

- 1 shot Southern Comfort
- Cranberry juice

Serve.

SCOOTER

- ¾ shot amaretto
- ¾ shot brandy
- 1 ounce cream

Shake.

SEVENTH HEAVEN

- ¾ shot Seagram's 7 whiskey
- ¼ shot amaretto
- Orange juice

Stir.

SHADY LADY

- ¾ shot tequila
- ¾ shot melon liqueur (Midori)
- Grapefruit juice
- Lime wedge and cherry slice

Garnish and serve.

SICILIAN KISS

- 1 shot Southern Comfort
- ½ shot amaretto

Stir.

SIDECAR

- 1 shot brandy
- ½ shot triple sec
- Splash of sour mix

Serve.

SINGAPORE SLING

- 1 shot gin
- ¼ shot cherry brandy
- Sour mix

- Splash of grenadine
- Soda water
- Cherry and orange slice

Shake first 4 ingredients, then add soda water. Garnish.

SIR WALTER RALEIGH

- 1 shot brandy
- ½ shot rum
- Dash of curaçao
- Dash of lime juice
- Dash of grenadine

Shake.

SLEDGEHAMMER

- ½ shot brandy
- ½ shot rum
- ½ shot apple brandy
- Dash of Pernod

Shake.

STONE SOUR

- 1 shot bourbon whiskey
- Dash of crème de menthe (white)
- Splash of lemon juice
- 1 teaspoon/packet sugar
- Soda water

Stir.

STONEWALL

- 1 shot dark rum
- Apple cider

Shake.

SWAMP WATER
- 1 shot rum
- ½ shot blue curaçao
- Orange juice
- Splash of lemon juice

Shake.

T.N.T.
- 1 shot tequila
- Tonic water
- Lime wedge

Garnish and serve.

TENNESSEE
- 1¼ shot rye whiskey
- ¼ shot Maraschino liqueur
- Splash of lemon juice

Shake.

TEQUINI
- 1⅛ shots tequila
- Dash of dry vermouth
- Lemon twist

Stir and garnish.

TIPPERARY
- ¾ shot Irish whiskey
- ¾ shot Chartreuse (green)
- ¾ shot sweet vermouth

Stir.

TOP BANANA
- ¾ shot vodka
- ¾ shot crème de banana
- Orange juice

Serve.

TOREADOR
- 1 shot tequila
- ½ shot crème de cacao (white)
- Splash of cream

Shake.

TRAFFIC LIGHT
- ½ shot crème de menthe (green)
- ½ shot crème de banana
- ½ shot sloe gin

Layer.

TROPICAL COCKTAIL
- ¾ shot crème de cacao (white)
- ¾ shot Maraschino liqueur
- ¾ shot sweet vermouth
- Dash of bitters

Stir.

VELVET HAMMER
- ½ shot crème de cacao (white)
- ½ shot triple sec
- 2 ounces cream

Shake.

VELVET KISS
- ¾ shot gin
- ¼ shot crème de banana
- 1 ounce cream
- Splash of pineapple juice

Shake.

VICTORY
- 1 shot Pernod
- Soda water
- Splash of grenadine

Serve.

VODKA COOLER

- ¾ shot vodka
- ¼ shot sweet vermouth
- Lemon-lime soda

Shake vodka and vermouth, then add lemon-lime soda.

VODKA GRAND MARNIER

- 1 shot vodka
- ¼ shot Grand Marnier
- Dash of lime juice
- Orange slice

Shake and garnish.

WARD EIGHT

- 1 shot bourbon whiskey
- Sour mix
- Splash of grenadine
- Cherry

Shake and garnish.

WHIRLAWAY

- 1 shot bourbon whiskey
- ½ shot curaçao
- Dash of bitters
- Soda water

Serve.

WILL ROGERS

- 1 shot gin
- ¼ shot dry vermouth
- Dash of triple sec
- Dash of orange juice

Shake.

XANTHIA

- ¾ shot Chartreuse (yellow)
- ¾ shot cherry brandy
- ¾ shot gin

Shake.

YELLOWBIRD

- ½ shot vodka
- ½ shot crème de cacao (white)
- ¼ shot Galliano
- Splash of orange juice
- Splash of cream

Shake.

YELLOW PARROT

- ½ shot anisette
- ½ shot apricot brandy
- ½ shot Chartreuse (yellow)

Shake.

ZOMBIE

- 1 shot rum
- 1 shot dark rum
- ¼ shot apricot brandy
- Orange juice
- Pineapple juice
- Splash of 151-proof rum floated on top
- Cherry and pineapple slice

Shake first 5 ingredients, then float 151-proof rum on top. Garnish and serve.

YOUR MIXED DRINKS
AND NOTES

FROZEN DRINKS

Most frozen drinks should be served in stemmed glasses. Not only do frozen drinks look better in these types of glasses, but more importantly, if held by the stem, the drink will stay cold longer. Because stemmed glasses come in many different sizes, make sure the glass you choose is large enough to hold the frozen drink. If it is not, you may have to alter the amount of ingredients you added to the mix. Unless otherwise noted, add approximately a cup of ice for each frozen drink. For a slushier drink, add more.

BANANA DAIQUIRI

- 1 shot rum
- Splash of crème de banana
- Splash of lime juice
- 1 teaspoon/packet sugar
- 1 ripe banana, sliced

Blend with ice.

BANANA SPLIT

- 1 shot crème de banana
- ¼ shot crème de cacao (white)
- ¼ shot crème de noyau
- Splash of milk
- Splash of grenadine

Blend with ice.

BAY BOMBER

- ¼ shot vodka
- ¼ shot gin
- ¼ shot rum
- ¼ shot tequila
- ¼ shot triple sec
- 1 ounce orange juice
- 1 ounce pineapple juice
- 1 ounce cranberry juice
- 1 ounce sour mix
- Splash of 151-proof rum floated on top

Blend liquors and juices with ice, then float 151-proof rum.

BLIZZARD

- 1 shot blended whiskey
- 2 ounces cranberry juice
- Dash of lemon juice
- 2 teaspoons/packets sugar

Blend with ice.

COOL OPERATOR

- ¾ shot melon liqueur (Midori)
- ¼ shot vodka
- ¼ shot rum
- Splash of lime juice
- 3 ounces grapefruit juice
- 3 ounces orange juice

Blend with ice.

DERBY DAIQUIRI

- 1 shot rum
- ½ shot Cointreau
- 1 ounce orange juice
- Splash of lime juice

Blend with about 3 ounces of ice.

FROZEN BIKINI

- 1 shot vodka
- ½ shot peach schnapps
- 2 ounces peach nectar
- 2 ounces orange juice
- Splash of lemon juice
- 1 ounce champagne (chilled)

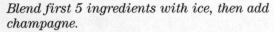

Blend first 5 ingredients with ice, then add champagne.

FROZEN FUZZY

- ¾ shot peach schnapps
- ¼ shot triple sec
- Splash of lime juice
- Splash of grenadine
- 1 ounce lemon-lime soda

Blend with ice.

FROZEN MATADOR

- 1 shot tequila
- 2 ounces pineapple juice
- Splash of lime juice

Blend with ice.

ICEBALL

- 1 shot gin
- ½ shot crème de menthe (white)
- ½ shot sambuca
- Splash of cream

Blend with ice.

ITALIAN BANANA

- ¾ shot amaretto
- ¾ shot crème de banana
- 2 ounces orange juice
- 1 ounce sour mix
- Cherry

Blend with ice and garnish.

JAMAICAN SHAKE

- 1 shot Myers's dark rum
- ½ shot blended whiskey
- 2 ounces milk or cream

Blend with ice.

MARASCHINO CHERRY

- ¾ shot rum
- ¼ shot amaretto
- ¼ shot peach schnapps
- 1 ounce cranberry juice
- 1 ounce pineapple juice
- Splash of grenadine
- Whipped Cream
- Cherry

Blend liquid ingredients with 2 cups of ice.
Top with whipped cream and a cherry.

MELON COLADA

- 1 shot rum
- ¼ shot melon liqueur (Midori)
- 4 ounces pineapple juice and 2 ounces coconut milk, OR 6 ounces piña colada mix
- Splash of cream
- Cherry

Blend with ice and garnish.

NUTTY COLADA

- 1½ shots amaretto
- 3 ounces pineapple juice and 2 ounces coconut milk, OR 5 ounces piña colada mix
- Splash of cream

Blend with ice.

PEACH DAIQUIRI

- 1 shot rum
- Splash of triple sec
- 1 ounce lime juice

Frozen Drinks 125

- 1 teaspoon/packet sugar
- ½ peach, sliced

Blend with ice.

SCORPION
- 1 shot rum
- ¼ shot brandy
- 2 ounces lemon juice
- 3 ounces orange juice
- Orange slice and cherry

Blend with ice and garnish.

SHARK BITE
- 1 shot dark rum
- Orange juice
- Splash of sour mix
- Splash of grenadine

Blend with ice.

SLOE TEQUILA
- ¾ shot tequila
- ¼ shot sloe gin
- Splash of lime juice

Blend with ice.

TIDAL WAVE
- ¾ shot melon liqueur (Midori)
- ¼ shot rum
- 1 ounce orange juice
- 2 ounces piña colada mix
- 2 ounces sour mix
- Cherry

Blend with ice and garnish.

TROPICAL STORM

- 1 shot dark rum
- ½ shot crème de banana
- 3 ounces orange juice
- Dash of grenadine
- ½ ripe banana, sliced
- Orange slice

Blend with ice and garnish.

YOUR FROZEN DRINKS
AND NOTES

ICE CREAM DRINKS

BLUE CLOUD

- ¾ shot amaretto
- ¼ shot blue curaçao
- 2 scoops vanilla ice cream
- Whipped cream
- Cherry

Blend first 3 ingredients, then top with whipped cream and cherry.

CARIBBEAN ICE CREAM

- ½ shot coffee-flavored liqueur (Kahlúa)
- ½ shot dark rum
- Splash of milk or cream
- 2 scoops vanilla ice cream

Blend.

CHOCOLATE BLACK RUSSIAN

- 1 shot vodka
- ½ shot coffee-flavored liqueur (Kahlúa)
- 2 scoops chocolate ice cream

Blend.

DREAMSICLE

- 1 shot amaretto
- Splash of milk or cream
- Splash of orange juice
- 2 scoops vanilla ice cream

Blend.

EMERALD ISLE

- ³/₄ shot Irish whiskey
- ³/₄ shot crème de menthe (green)
- 2 scoops vanilla ice cream
- Soda water

Blend first 3 ingredients, then add soda water. Stir after adding soda water.

FROZEN CAPPUCCINO

- ½ shot Irish cream
- ¼ shot coffee-flavored liqueur (Kahlúa)
- ¼ shot hazelnut liqueur (Frangelico)
- Splash of cream
- 1 scoop vanilla ice cream

Blend with ½ cup of ice.

INTERNATIONAL CREAM

- ½ shot Irish cream
- ½ shot coffee-flavored liqueur (Kahlúa)
- Splash of Grand Marnier
- 2 scoops vanilla ice cream
- Splash of milk

Blend.

MISSISSIPPI MUD

- ³/₄ shot Southern Comfort
- ³/₄ shot coffee-flavored liqueur (Kahlúa)
- 2 scoops vanilla ice cream

Blend.

NUT 'N' CREAM

- ½ shot amaretto
- ½ shot hazelnut liqueur (Frangelico)
- 2 scoops vanilla ice cream
- Splash of milk
- Grated nutmeg

Blend first 4 ingredients, then dust with grated nutmeg.

ADULT ROOT BEER FLOAT

- ½ shot coffee-flavored liqueur (Kahlúa)
- ½ shot Galliano
- 2 scoops vanilla ice cream
- Cola

*Blend first 3 ingredients, then add cola.
Stir after adding cola.*

RUSSIAN ICE

- 1 shot Stolichnaya (Russian vodka)
- ½ shot coffee-flavored liqueur (Kahlúa)
- Splash of cream
- 2 scoops vanilla ice cream

Blend.

STRAWBERRY SHORTCAKE

- ¾ shot crème de noyau
- ¼ shot crème de cacao (white)
- 2 scoops vanilla ice cream
- 6 strawberries
- Whipped cream
- Splash of strawberry liqueur

*Blend first 4 ingredients, add whipped
cream, and top it off with strawberry
liqueur.*

YOUR ICE CREAM DRINKS
AND NOTES

HOT DRINKS

Hot drinks can be a real hit, especially after a long day of skiing or on a cold and stormy night. They are relatively easy to make, and because of the popularity of most hot mixers (i.e. hot chocolate, coffee, etc.) these drinks appeal to a wide range of tastes. To insure their enjoyment, there are a few safety tips which should be followed when serving these drinks.

The cups these drinks are served in should be heated under warm water prior to the addition of the hot drink. Also, because of its superior heat conductivity, it's a good idea to place a metal spoon in the glass or cup to prevent the container from cracking when the hot drink is poured. And finally, be aware that hot drinks can heat a metallic mug in a very short period of time, creating the possibility of burns to the lips of an unsuspecting drinker.

ADULT HOT CHOCOLATE

- 1 shot peppermint schnapps
- Hot chocolate
- Whipped cream

Top with whipped cream and serve.

AMARETTO CAFÉ

- 1 shot amaretto
- Hot black coffee
- Whipped cream

Top with whipped cream and serve.

BAILEYS AND COFFEE

- 1 shot Baileys Irish Cream
- Hot black coffee
- Whipped cream

Top with whipped cream and serve.

COMFORTABLE FIRE

- 1 shot Southern Comfort
- Hot apple cider
- Cinnamon stick

Garnish and serve.

COMFORTABLE MOCHA

- 1 shot Southern Comfort
- Hot chocolate
- Hot black coffee

Serve.

FUZZY NUT

- 1 shot peach schnapps
- ¼ shot amaretto
- Hot chocolate
- Whipped cream

Top with whipped cream and serve.

GROG

- 1 shot rum
- 1 teaspoon/packet sugar
- Dash of lime juice
- Boiling water
- Cinnamon stick

Stir.

HOT BUTTERED RUM

- 1½ shots dark rum
- 1 teaspoon/packet sugar
- 1 teaspoon butter

- Boiling water
- Grated nutmeg

Stir and dust with nutmeg.

HOT GOLD

- 1 shot amaretto
- Warm orange juice
- Cinnamon stick

Garnish and serve.

HOT NAIL

- 1 shot Scotch whisky
- ½ shot Drambuie
- Dash of lemon juice
- Boiling water
- Lemon slice and cinnamon stick

Garnish and serve.

HOT PEPPERMINT PATTY

- 1 shot peppermint schnapps
- Hot chocolate
- Splash of milk
- Whipped cream

Top with whipped cream and serve.

HOT TODDY

- 1 shot blended whiskey
- 1 teaspoon/packet sugar
- Boiling water
- Grated nutmeg
- Cinnamon stick

Stir first 3 ingredients, dust with nutmeg, and garnish with cinnamon stick.

HOUSE FIRE

- 1 shot amaretto
- Hot apple cider
- Cinnamon stick

Garnish and serve.

JAMAICAN COFFEE

- ³⁄₄ shot Tia Maria
- ³⁄₄ shot Jamaican rum
- Hot black coffee
- Whipped cream

Top with whipped cream and serve.

KAHLÚA AND COFFEE

- 1 shot coffee-flavored liqueur (Kahlúa)
- Hot black coffee
- Whipped cream

Top with whipped cream and serve.

KAHLÚA AND HOT CHOCOLATE

- 1 shot coffee-flavored liqueur (Kahlúa)
- Hot chocolate
- Whipped cream

Top with whipped cream and serve.

KIOKI COFFEE

- ³⁄₄ shot coffee-flavored liqueur (Kahlúa)
- ¹⁄₄ shot brandy
- Hot black coffee

Serve.

MALIBU CAFÉ

- 1 shot Malibu rum
- Hot black coffee
- Whipped cream

Top with whipped cream and serve.

MARNIER CAFÉ

- 1 shot Grand Marnier
- Hot black coffee
- Whipped cream

Top with whipped cream and serve.

MEXICAN CAFÉ
- ¾ shot coffee-flavored liqueur (Kahlúa)
- ¼ shot tequila
- Hot black coffee

Serve.

NUTTY CAFÉ
- ¾ shot amaretto
- ¼ shot hazelnut liqueur (Frangelico)
- Hot black coffee
- Whipped cream

Top with whipped cream and serve.

SWEET DREAMS
- 1 shot rum
- 1 teaspoon/packet sugar
- Warm milk
- Grated nutmeg

Dust with nutmeg and serve.

TEA GROG
- ¾ shot dark rum
- ¾ shot brandy
- 1 teaspoon honey
- Hot tea
- Cinnamon stick

Stir and add cinnamon stick.

TOM AND JERRY
- 1 egg, separated
- 2 teaspoons/2 packets sugar
- Pinch of baking soda
- ¾ shot dark rum
- ¾ shot brandy
- Hot milk
- Grated nutmeg

Beat egg and yolk separately. Fold together combining with sugar and baking soda in a heatproof mug. Mix in dark rum and brandy. Fill with hot milk. Dust with nutmeg.

Hot Drinks　　　　　　　　　　　　**137**

ALCOHOL-FREE DRINKS

BEACH BLANKET BINGO
- Cranberry juice
- Grape juice
- Splash of soda water

Serve.

BLACK COW
- 2 scoops of vanilla ice cream
- Root beer

Serve.

CAFÉ MOCHA
- Hot black coffee
- Hot chocolate
- Whipped cream

Top with whipped cream and serve.

CRANBERRY COOLER
- 3 ounces cranberry juice
- Splash of lime juice
- Soda water

Serve.

DIRTY WATER
- Root beer
- Orange soda

Stir.

GENTLE SEA BREEZE

- Grapefruit juice
- Cranberry juice
- Lime wedge

Stir and garnish.

GRAPEBERRY

- Cranberry juice
- Grapefruit juice
- Lime wedge

Garnish and serve.

GREAT GRAPE

- 3 ounces grape juice
- Cranberry juice
- Sour mix
- Lemon-lime soda

Serve.

JUICE COOLER

- Cranberry juice
- Grapefruit juice
- Orange juice
- Pineapple juice
- Ginger ale or soda water

Serve.

JUICER

- Cranberry juice
- Grapefruit juice
- Orange juice
- Pineapple juice

Serve.

LIME COOLER

- Dash of lime juice
- Cola
- Lime wedge

Garnish and serve.

LIMONADE

- 2 ounces sour mix
- Lemon-lime soda
- Soda water
- Lemon slice and lime wedge

Garnish and serve.

NO RUM RICKEY

- 1 ounce lime juice
- Splash of bitters
- Splash of grenadine
- Soda water
- Lime wedge

Garnish and serve.

ORANGE AND TONIC

- Orange juice
- Tonic water
- Orange slice

Garnish and serve.

ORGEAT COCKTAIL

- 1 egg white
- 1 ounce lemon juice
- ¾ ounce orgeat syrup
- Cherry

Shake and garnish.

PAC-MAN

- Ginger ale
- Dash of lemon juice
- Dash of bitters
- Dash of grenadine
- Orange slice and cherry

Garnish and serve.

PLANTER'S JUICE

- Pineapple juice
- Orange juice
- Splash of lime juice

- 1 teaspoon/packet sugar
- Splash of coconut milk
- Splash of grenadine
- Soda water
- Cherry and orange slice

Garnish and serve.

RASP-MA-TAZZ
- 6 ounces pineapple juice
- 1 dozen raspberries (or 6 strawberries, if desired)
- 1 ripe banana

Blend with ice.

ROY ROGERS
- Dash of grenadine
- Cola
- Cherry

Garnish and serve.

SHIRLEY TEMPLE
- Ginger ale
- Dash of grenadine
- Cherry

Garnish and serve.

SOBER DRIVER
- Splash of club soda
- Orange juice

Serve.

SOBER SPRITZER
- 3 ounces white grape juice
- Soda water

Serve.

TEQUILA SUNSET
- Orange juice
- Dash of grenadine

Serve.

TOMATO AND TONIC

- 3 ounces tonic water
- Tomato juice
- Lime wedge

Garnish and serve.

TRANSFUSION

- 3 ounces grape juice
- Ginger ale
- Dash of lime juice
- Lime wedge

Garnish and serve.

UNFUZZY NAVEL

- Peach nectar
- Orange juice
- Dash of lemon juice
- Dash of grenadine
- Orange slice

Garnish and serve.

VANILLA COLA

- Splash of vanilla extract (trace amounts of alcohol)
- Cola

Serve.

VIRGIN COLADA

- Pineapple juice
- Coconut milk
- Pineapple slice and cherry

Blend with ice and garnish.

VIRGIN CREAMSICLE

- 2 scoops vanilla ice cream
- 6 ounces orange juice
- Dash of almond extract or orgeat syrup

Blend.

VIRGIN EGGNOG

- 1 egg
- 1 teaspoon/packet sugar
- Dash of vanilla extract (trace amounts of alcohol)
- 1 cup milk
- Grated nutmeg

Beat the egg and sugar, then add the vanilla extract and milk. Pour into empty highball glass (no ice). Dust with nutmeg.

YOUR ALCOHOL-FREE
DRINKS AND NOTES

EGGNOGS AND PUNCHES

Eggnog can be made either by using a prepared eggnog mix or by mixing the raw ingredients. The advantage of using a prepared eggnog mix is that salmonella is much less of a threat than when using raw eggs. If you choose to mix the raw ingredients, do so by separating the eggs (yolk from white), and beating the yolk with sugar until it is thick. Then gradually stir in the liquor followed by the milk and cream. In another bowl, beat egg whites until stiff. Keep both mixes refrigerated separately until well-chilled and ready to serve. When ready to serve, carefully fold egg whites in with rest of mix. Be careful not to beat or stir. Never add ice to eggnog. The eggnog recipes below contain approximately ten to twelve servings; increase the ingredients proportionately to yield a greater number of servings.

With a party of twenty or more people punch can be a real crowd-pleaser while saving you both time and money. A punch can be made prior to the party and, once made (as long as you do not run out of it), you can let your guests serve themselves. Depending on the occasion, you can serve a punch in place of a full bar, or at least provide a limited bar when serving punch. Punch and eggnog are especially appropriate around the holidays, but punch can add a special touch to a party at any time during the year.

Because punch will normally be tried by all, young and old, and at times can look so innocent, its strength is something which you must take into account when making. Consider the ages of those at the party and the time of day of the party. If, for example, you were serving a punch for a party in celebration of a graduation from high school, odds are the punch will be consumed by young people, so a weak punch would be advisable.

Punch is relatively easy to make, but there are a few guidelines to follow when making. To cool punch, use one or more large blocks of ice, never ice cubes. Because of the decreased surface area of an ice block, it will dissolve at a much slower rate than ice cubes, therefore keeping the punch colder without diluting it. To make a block of ice, simply fill a large container with water and freeze. You can be creative when making ice blocks by using molds with different designs as is done with Jell-O. Because punch is typically made well before it is served, make sure all carbonated beverages are only added just prior to your guests' arrival, otherwise the punch will go flat. The amount each punch recipe yields is based on 4 ounces per serving.

EGGNOGS

BALTIMORE EGGNOG
- 1 quart prepared eggnog mix; OR 5 eggs
- 16 ounces milk
- 5 ounces cream
- 5 ounces superfine sugar
- 5 ounces brandy
- 5 ounces dark rum
- 5 ounces peach brandy or Madeira wine
- Grated nutmeg

Dust nutmeg over each serving.

BREAKFAST EGGNOG

- 1 quart prepared eggnog mix; OR 5 eggs
- 15 ounces milk
- 5 ounces cream
- 5 ounces superfine sugar
- 10 ounces brandy
- 2 ounces triple sec
- Grated nutmeg

Dust nutmeg over each serving.

EGGNOG (BASIC)

- 1 quart prepared eggnog mix; OR 5 eggs
- 15 ounces milk
- 5 ounces cream
- 5 ounces superfine sugar
- 6 ounces cognac
- 6 ounces dark rum
- Grated nutmeg

Dust nutmeg over each serving.

PUNCHES

BOMBAY PUNCH

- 12 lemons
- Sugar to taste
- One 750-ml. bottle brandy
- One 750-ml. bottle dry sherry
- 4 ounces Maraschino liqueur
- 4 ounces curaçao
- Four 750-ml. bottles champagne
- 2 quarts soda water
- Variety of sliced fruit

Prechill all ingredients. Squeeze lemons into container and mix with enough sugar to sweeten. Pour juice/sugar mix over large block/s of ice in punch bowl and stir in brandy, sherry, Maraschino liqueur, and curaçao. Just prior to serving, gently stir in champagne and soda water. Garnish with fruit slices and serve in punch glasses.

Approximately 60 servings

BRANDY PUNCH

- 12 lemons
- 4 oranges
- Sugar to taste
- 8 ounces curaçao
- Two 750-ml. bottles brandy
- 8 ounces grenadine
- 1 quart soda water, OR one 750-ml. bottle champagne
- Variety of sliced fruit

Prechill all ingredients. Squeeze lemons and oranges into container and mix with enough sugar to sweeten. Pour juice/sugar mix over large block/s of ice in punch bowl. Stir in brandy, curaçao, and grenadine. Just prior to serving, gently stir in either one or a combination of both soda water and champagne. Garnish with fruit slices and serve in punch glasses.

Approximately 35 servings

BUDDHA PUNCH

- One 750-ml. bottle Rhine wine
- 4 ounces curaçao
- 4 ounces rum
- 8 ounces orange juice
- Several dashes of angostura bitters
- 1 quart soda water
- One 750-ml. bottle champagne
- Variety of sliced fruit

Prechill all ingredients. Add all ingredients except soda water and champagne into a punch bowl with block/s of ice. Just prior to serving, gently stir in soda water and

*champagne. Garnish with fruit slices and
serve in punch glasses.*

Approximately 25 servings

CARDINAL PUNCH

- 12 lemons
- Sugar to taste
- Two 750-ml. bottles dry red wine
- 16 ounces brandy
- 16 ounces rum
- 3 ounces sweet vermouth
- 2 quarts soda water
- One 750-ml. bottle champagne
- Variety of sliced fruit

*Prechill all ingredients. Squeeze lemons into
container and mix with enough sugar to
sweeten. Pour juice/sugar mix over large
block/s of ice into punch bowl. Stir in wine,
brandy, rum, and vermouth. Just prior to
serving, gently stir in either one or a
combination of both soda water and chilled
champagne. Garnish with fruit slices and
serve in punch glasses.*

Approximately 50 servings

CHAMPAGNE PUNCH

- 12 lemons
- Sugar to taste
- 16 ounces brandy
- 8 ounces curaçao
- 16 ounces soda water
- Two 750-ml. bottles champagne
- Variety of fruit slices

*Prechill all ingredients. Squeeze lemons into
container and mix with enough sugar to
sweeten. Pour juice/sugar mix over large
block/s of ice into punch bowl. Stir in brandy
and curaçao. Just prior to serving, gently stir
in soda water and champagne. Garnish with
fruit slices and serve in punch glasses.*

Approximately 30 servings

CHAMPAGNE SHERBET PUNCH

- 24 ounces pineapple juice
- 2 ounces lemon juice
- One 750-ml. bottle champagne
- 1 quart lemon, pineapple, or other flavored sherbet

Prechill all ingredients. Stir juices over large block/s of ice. Just prior to serving gently stir in champagne and scoop in sherbet.

Approximately 20 servings

CLARET PUNCH

- 12 lemons
- Sugar to taste
- Two 750-ml. bottles claret
- 16 ounces brandy
- 8 ounces curaçao
- 2 quarts soda water
- Variety of sliced fruit

Prechill all ingredients. Squeeze lemons into container and mix with enough sugar to sweeten. Pour juice/sugar mix over large block/s of ice in punch bowl. Stir in claret, brandy, and curaçao. Just prior to serving, gently stir in soda water. Garnish with fruits of your choice and serve in punch glasses.

Approximately 40 servings

FISH HOUSE PUNCH

- 12 lemons
- Sugar to taste
- One 750-ml. bottle brandy
- 4 ounces peach brandy
- 16 ounces rum
- 2 quarts soda water or flavored soda (cola, 7-Up, or ginger ale)
- Variety of sliced fruit

Prechill all ingredients. Squeeze lemons into container and mix with enough sugar to sweeten. Pour juice/sugar mix over large

---

block/s of ice in punch bowl. Stir in brandies and rum. Just prior to serving, gently stir in desired soda. Garnish with fruit slices and serve in punch glasses.

Approximately 35 servings

SANGRIA

As with other punches, there are many variations of Sangria. You may want to experiment with various ingredients and combinations of them to arrive at the Sangria you like best.

- Two 750-ml. bottles red wine
- 8 ounces rum
- 16 ounces orange juice
- 16 ounces pineapple juice
- 30 ounces canned fruit cocktail
- 1 quart soda water or ginger ale
- Variety of sliced fruit

Prechill all ingredients. Stir all ingredients except soda water or ginger ale over large block/s of ice in punch bowl. Just prior to serving, gently stir in soda of choice. Garnish with fruits and serve in red wine glasses.

Approximately 40 servings

TEQUILA PUNCH

- 1 liter tequila
- Four 750-ml. bottles Sauterne
- 2 quarts various fresh fruit balls and cubes
- One 750-ml. bottle champagne

Prechill all ingredients. Stir tequila and Sauterne into a punch bowl over large block/s of ice. Add various fresh fruit cut into balls and cubes. Just prior to serving, gently stir in champagne. Serve in punch cups.

Approximately 55 servings

WHISKEY PUNCH

- 6 lemons
- Two 750-ml. bottles bourbon or blended whiskey
- 4 ounces curaçao
- 1 quart apple juice
- 2 ounces grenadine
- 4 quarts soda water or ginger ale
- Cherries

Prechill all ingredients. Squeeze lemons into punch bowl over large block/s of ice. Stir in whiskey, curaçao, juice, and grenadine. Just prior to serving, gently stir in soda of choice. Garnish with cherries. Serve in punch glasses.

Approximately 60 servings

WHISKEY SOUR PUNCH

- One 750-ml. bottle bourbon or blended whiskey
- 18 ounces frozen lemonade concentrate (thawed and undiluted)
- 24 ounces orange juice
- 2 quarts soda water
- Orange slices and cherries

Prechill all ingredients. Stir all ingredients except soda water in punch bowl over large block/s of ice. Just prior to serving, gently stir in soda water. Garnish. Serve in punch glasses.

Approximately 35 servings

HOT PUNCHES

BANDIT'S BREW

- 12 ounces dark rum
- 1 quart tea
- 3 tablespoons butter
- 4 ounces sugar
- ½ teaspoon grated nutmeg
- 4 ounces brandy

Heat all ingredients except brandy in a saucepan until mix boils. Heat brandy in separate saucepan until it is warm; add brandy to mix. Serve punch in heatproof glasses.

Approximately 12 servings

GLÜG

- 8 ounces water
- 1 cup raisins
- 15 cardamom seeds
- 3 cinnamon sticks
- 4 cloves
- 2 dry orange peels

Boil the above ingredients for 10 to 15 minutes in saucepan. Add following ingredients to the mix and boil entire mix.

- 4 quarts port wine
- One 750-ml. bottle brandy
- 16 ounces rum
- ½ cup sugar

Let mix boil for around a minute then turn off burner and ignite the mix. Allow the mix to burn for about 15 seconds. Serve hot in punch glasses.

Approximately 50 servings

HOT APPLE BRANDY

- 1½ quarts apple juice
- 3 cinnamon sticks
- ½ teaspoon ground cloves
- 12 ounces apricot brandy

In a saucepan, simmer all ingredients except for apricot brandy over low heat. Add apricot brandy to mix after it has simmered for 15 minutes, and allow to simmer for an additional 15 minutes (total of 30 minutes). Serve warm in brandy snifters.

Approximately 15 servings

HOT APPLE RUM PUNCH

- 1 liter dark rum
- 1 quart apple cider
- 3 broken cinnamon sticks
- 1½ tablespoons butter

Heat all ingredients in saucepan until mix almost boils. Serve punch hot in heatproof glasses.

Approximately 15 servings

ALCOHOL-FREE PUNCHES

JUNGLE JUICE

- One 12-ounce can frozen orange juice concentrate, thawed and undiluted
- One 12-ounce can frozen lemonade concentrate, thawed and undiluted
- One 12-ounce can frozen grape juice concentrate, thawed and undiluted
- 2¼ quarts water
- 1 quart ginger ale
- 1 pint raspberry sherbet

Prechill all ingredients. Stir concentrates and water over large ice block/s in a punch bowl. Just prior to serving, gently stir ginger ale in and spoon sherbet on top of punch. Serve in punch glasses.

Approximately 40 servings

PINEBERRY PUNCH

- 2 quarts pineapple juice
- 2 quarts cranberry juice
- 16 ounces soda water
- 16 ounces ginger ale
- Variety of sliced fruit

Prechill all ingredients. Stir juices over ice block/s in punch bowl. Just prior to serving, gently stir in sodas. Garnish with fruit slices.

Approximately 40 servings

RAINBOW PUNCH

- 8 ounces orange juice
- 8 ounces pineapple juice
- 8 ounces red Hawaiian Punch
- 1 quart soda water
- 1 quart ginger ale
- 1 quart rainbow sherbet

Prechill all ingredients. Stir juices and punch over ice block/s in a punch bowl. Just prior to serving, gently stir in sodas and spoon sherbet on top of punch. Serve in punch glasses.

Approximately 30 servings

VERRY BERRY PUNCH

- 12 raspberries
- 2 quarts cranberry juice
- 24 ounces raspberry soda
- 1 quart raspberry sherbet

Prechill all ingredients. Stir raspberries and cranberry juice over ice block/s in a punch bowl. Just prior to serving, gently stir in raspberry soda and spoon sherbet on top of punch. Serve in punch glasses.

Approximately 30 servings

APPENDIX 1
POINTERS FROM
THE PRO

ICE

Never scoop ice with the glass that you will serve a drink in. Always use an ice scoop or a shaker, never a glass object. There are two reasons for this. First, it looks very unsanitary—patrons may think, correctly or not, that you are filling unclean glasses directly from the ice bin. This impression comes from the fact that patrons often prefer their glasses to be refilled using the old ice rather than receiving their next drink in a clean, empty glass (it is said that alcohol gets concentrated in ice). Second and more importantly, it is very easy to break glass in the ice bin. When this happens, and eventually it will, you *must* empty all the ice from the bin. Then, clean the bin with hot water and a rag, to get all of the broken glass. Then refill the bin with ice. This is a very time-consuming procedure, so get in the habit of using a scoop.

BLEEDING

If a specific beer or wine tap, or the soda gun, has not been used for a few hours its line should be bled. Bleeding a line is simply running the line to clear the beer, wine, or soda which collects there. The liquid that sits in the lines becomes stale after a few hours, and thus needs to be dumped. This is important because stale beer, wine which has become vinegar, or flat soda is not a pleasant drink.

THE CALLING ORDER

A calling order is a system where the waitress orders drinks from the bartender in a specific chronological order. Many bars do not practice a calling order, although it is something all bars should utilize. A calling order limits confusion and speeds the entire ordering process.

For example, a typical calling order might be as follows: 1) mixed drinks; 2) soft drinks; 3) wine; 4) beer; 5) shots. This means that if the order was a glass of red wine, a shot of sambuca, four bottles of Miller Genuine Draft (beer), and two Vodka and Tonics, the waitress would not simply order it in the above miscellaneous fashion, but rather in the proper calling order. For this particular drink order we will use the calling order we have listed above. The waitress should begin the order by saying "ordering," then stating any mixed drinks followed by the number of these drinks—in this case two times—then stating any soft drinks, the number of each, and so on. Stating the number of each drink after the drink is much easier to remember, and though it may not sound so, is much less confusing than stating the number followed by the drink.

Her complete order would sound like this: "ORDERING, vodka tonic two times, Genuine Draft four times, red wine one glass, sambuca one shot." It cannot be stressed enough how much easier a bartender's night can be if a calling order is practiced. It makes the entire process, from remembering what was ordered to calculating the order's total price, much easier.

TIPS

A great number of the tips a bartender receives are $1 bills. Often, especially on busy nights, the register will run out of these bills. Therefore, instead of stuffing your bills into a jar, as most bartenders do, it is a good idea to either lay them flat, one on top of another, or keep them in a jar or pitcher in an orderly fashion. If and when the register runs out of singles, you are ready with a reserve stack. Don't forget to reimburse your tip jar equitably with larger bills from the same register in which you placed the singles.

There are many tricks for increasing your tips, including laying out a couple of $1 bills on the bar. (This is supposed to catch your patrons' eyes and remind them to tip.) Some bartenders are always ready to light a patron's cigarette, others have their regular customers' drinks waiting for them as they sit down. These may or may not work, but the only guaranteed way to increase your tips (other than simply making good drinks and being polite) is keeping the bar clean. This means emptying ashtrays with one or more cigarette butts. The bar should be wiped down frequently, as liquid, napkins, and cigarette wrappers collect upon it. This also means keeping glasses clean; lipstick and other stains are *very* noticeable on glass if not removed, and will definitely hurt your tips.

SERVING

If there are both women and men in a group, it is proper to serve the women their drinks before the men.

Drinks served to patrons seated at the bar should be accompanied by a napkin or coaster.

If someone asks for a chilled beer glass or liquor glass (most notably the cocktail glass), this can be done even if you have not planned ahead or do not have space in the cooler to chill glasses. Place the glass to be chilled in a bucket or large pitcher with ice, cover the glass with ice, and spin the glass for approximately 20 to 30 seconds. The glass will be properly chilled enough to have condensation on its sides.

Many bars lack ginger ale in the soda gun. This is no problem. Ginger ale can be made very easily if the gun has lemon-lime soda (7-Up or Sprite) and cola. Simply fill the glass almost all the way to the top with lemon-lime soda, then add a little more than a splash of cola. Stir it gently and *voilà:* ginger ale.

When making a drink calling for two primary mixers, both of which are available on the soda gun, push the buttons for both mixers simultaneously. The glass will fill faster and contain exactly half of each of the mixers (for example, Seabreeze, which has cranberry and grapefruit juice as its primary mixers).

If there is enough room in either the cooler or the ice bin, put in bottles of your bar's most popular shots which are served chilled. Doing this will save valuable time which would otherwise be used chilling those shots. It is also smart, and in many bars a necessity, to keep premixed bottles of Watermelon and Kamikaze shots. Due to the fruit juices they contain, these shots are perishable, and the bottles must be kept cold.

IMPROVISING

When you get behind the bar, you will realize that oftentimes you won't have certain tools of the trade, and therefore must improvise. The absence of proper tools may be due to bartenders not replacing them where they belong. If you've been asked to make a chilled drink and you can't find the strainer, simply chill the liquid in either a glass or a shaker and then place an empty glass right side up into the mix. Hold both the glass and the container and begin pouring slowly into the shot or cocktail glass. The empty glass will work as a strainer and hold the ice while allowing the liquid to flow around the edges. In order to be ready for the necessity of using this technique, practice with water before pouring with liquor.

POURING BEER

Many new bartenders have difficulty pouring draft beers, and allow too much head to form on the beer. New bartenders often think a bar keg is just like a party keg, and all one needs to do is tilt the glass while pouring to eliminate the foam. This is not the case, because bar kegs are better refrigerated and are powered by carbon dioxide. The key to pouring beer from a bar tapper is to allow the first squirt from the tapper (usually foam) to miss the glass, then to capture the rest of the beer with the glass touching the metal spout. The glass should be tilted at about 15 degrees, and gradually the angle should increase until the glass is full and upright. The beer should have about a half inch of head.

MISCELLANEOUS

If for any reason it becomes necessary to taste a patron's drink, usually to check its contents, it can be done easily and sanitarily. Simply submerge a straw or mixing rod into the drink, then place your finger over the top of the device; enough liquid will be captured in the straw to taste test. Do not double dip with the same straw!

When pouring a drink from a bottle of liquor which is almost empty, always use a jigger. If the bottle empties perfectly at a shot, the patron, if watching, will feel shortchanged. If it empties at under a shot, your count will be off. Fill the jigger with the contents from two bottles and you won't risk disappointing the customer.

If someone orders a drink, usually a shot, and requests a chaser, the chaser is generally at no charge. The chaser, usually cola, should be served without ice in the small rocks glass.

Whenever someone orders a nonalcoholic beer, always offer the patron a glass. Many people are self-conscious about drinking nonalcoholic beer in a bar.

Because a speed rack is often used without consciously looking at the bottle which is poured, it is a good idea to divide bottles by appearance. For example, split the vodka and gin bottles by placing a whiskey bottle between them. This should be done because vodka and gin look alike and many times you will not have time to look at the label. You will quickly notice the mistake if you grab a dark bottle of whiskey rather than a clear bottle of either gin or vodka.

The practice of stirring a patron's drink has for the most part been phased out. If a bartender is pouring mixers from a soda gun, he or she does not need to stir a patron's drink, even if the mixer is un-carbonated. The pressure of the mixer coming from the soda gun will mix the drink.

It is very important to clean both shaker shells and the strainer after each use. An unclean shaker and strainer will taint future drinks.

If you are out of Seagram's 7 or Jack Daniel's and someone orders a 7&7, or a Jack and Coke, do not reach for a substitute or for bar whiskey to complete the order. Simply by ordering these drinks, the customer is making a "call" order. Suggest a similar brand or tell him or her what brands are stocked. If the patron sees you pouring something other than the brand requested, he or she has a right to complain.

When making any drink calling for the rim to be salted, the rim must be dampened in order for the salt to stick to it. Dampen the rim by taking a lime and rubbing it around the glass's rim. Then take the glass and spin it in the salt. The glass is now ready for the drink.

When opening a bottle of wine with a corkscrew, make sure the corkscrew does not pierce the opposite end of the cork. If the corkscrew pushes through the entire cork, it will break the cork, sending pieces of cork into the wine. This is a pet peeve for many wine drinkers, especially those having to remove small pieces of cork from expensive wine.

If you need crushed or shaved ice yet have no access to an electric ice-crusher, you have two options. You can either use an electric blender or crush the ice by hand. If you decide to use an electric blender you should be aware that, unless you have a very heavy-duty model with a sharp blade, crushing ice in your blender could damage it. Remember when making frozen drinks that you have quite a bit of liquid mix, which will act as a catalyst in the process, thereby taking some strain off of your blender. To crush ice by hand, simply fill a plastic bag with ice and wrap a towel around the bag. Then place the bag and towel on a counter or table and crush the ice either with a rolling pin (by rolling over the bag) or by hitting the bag with a blunt object such as a mallet, hammer, or the barrel end of a bat.

Some people make opening champagne a major job, but if done correctly, it is a simple task. Instead of fighting to twist and pull the champagne cork, hold the cork firmly with one hand while twisting the bottle with the other hand. When removing a cork, always point the bottle away from everyone, including yourself.

APPENDIX 2
BAR
TERMINOLOGY

Call: When a patron specifies the brand of alcohol to be used in his or her drink. For instance, if someone ordered a Tanqueray and Tonic instead of a Gin and Tonic, this would be a *call* drink. Whenever either call or top-shelf liquor is requested, the patron has ordered a call drink. Never use any brand but the brand called; if you are out of that brand, let the patron know what brands in the desired category you do have.

Chaser: Sometimes called a "side" or a "back," this is a mixer which is served in a separate glass and consumed just after a shot. A chaser masks the often harsh taste of the shot. Cola is the most frequently requested chaser.

Collins: A class of drinks including John Collins (whiskey), Rum Collins, Tequila Collins, the ever-famous Tom Collins (gin), and the Vodka Collins. This class of drinks made in the collins glass consists of the specified liquor, sour mix, club soda, and a cherry. The names of the different Collins drinks represent the liquors used in the making.

Comp: Short for complimentary drink. The house or bartender will often "comp" the patron a drink. Most bars have policies on complimentary drinks. Check the policy of your bar.

Dash: This refers to a quantity of liquid. A dash is technically about one-sixth of a teaspoon, or several drops. Those ingredients which often only require a dash (bitters, Tabasco, etc.), have pourers which allow this amount to be dispensed by giving the bottle a quick flip over the drink.

Double: A drink requested with double the amount of liquor that is served in the normal version of that drink. For example, a double Rum and Coke would contain two shots of rum instead of just one.

Dry: This refers to the amount of dry vermouth added to a Martini. The less dry vermouth added to a Martini, the drier it is. An Extra Dry Martini has just a trace of dry vermouth.

Garbage: Any garnish that does not improve the taste of the drink it is placed in. In other words, the purpose of "garbage" is to make the drink look better. Examples of garbage are a celery stalk in a Bloody Mary or a Maraschino cherry in a Manhattan.

Mixer: Any nonalcoholic liquid mixed with alcohol in a drink.

Neat: Any shot of liquor or liqueur which is consumed by itself without ice is "neat." For example, if someone ordered a shot of whiskey neat, he or she would be ordering a shot of whiskey in a shot glass, unchilled.

Perfect: This is a term used with drinks calling for vermouth. Any drink calling for vermouth, either dry or sweet, can be made perfect by adding equal parts of both dry and sweet vermouth. For example, a Perfect Manhattan contains not only sweet vermouth, but an equal portion of dry vermouth.

Proof: Refers to the percent of alcohol in a given beverage. This number is derived from a scale wherein 200 is equal to 100 percent alcohol. Therefore, a bottle containing liquor which is 86 proof is in fact 43 percent alcohol (divide proof by two to arrive at the percent of alcohol). The proof of a beverage is printed on the labels of all liquor bottles.

Short: This term is used in reference to "underpouring" a drink, or pouring less than the required amount of alcohol. It is not an accepted bartending practice. A good rule of thumb is: never short the customer (underpour) or the house (overpour).

Splash: This refers to a quantity of liquid. A splash is a little less than ½ ounce. Those ingredients that often only require a splash (such as lime juice, grenadine, and so on) have pourers allowing this amount to be easily dispensed. You should learn to dispense a splash by simply giving the bottle a quick squirt over the drink.

Tall: A patron will order a "tall" when he or she wants the given drink served in a tall glass. This request is usually made when the drink is normally served in a small rocks glass. A tall is ordered because the patron wants a greater quantity of mixer than can be added to a small rocks glass. Remember, only add more mixer in a tall; the amount of liquor stays the same.

Twist: A "twist" or a "twist of lemon" is a piece of lemon peel. A twist should be a rectangular piece approximately 1 inch by ¼ inch. It is called a "twist" because it is twisted above the drink before it is added to the drink. To impart more of the peel's taste to the drink, rub the twist along the rim of the glass. Though the peels of fruits other than the lemon are used to garnish drinks, their use is very infrequent. Often, when patrons order a drink such as Vodka and Tonic with a "twist of lime," they mean a lime wedge; most customers are simply not up on the proper bar lingo.

Virgin: A drink made without liquor. A Virgin Mary is an example of a virgin drink; it contains all the ingredients of a Bloody Mary except the vodka.

APPENDIX 3
BARTENDING
AT HOME

Have you ever wondered why drinks taste so much better at a bar than they do at home or at un-catered parties? In this section we will discuss the difference between drinks made in a bar and drinks made at home so you will be able to make drinks which taste, feel, and look every bit as good as those made by the pros.

The most obvious problem with most drinks made at home is that often incorrect quantities of al-cohol and mixers are used. As explained on page 9, a shot is an unregulated amount, usually around an ounce. Because this quantity is arbitrary, and, for the sake of consistency, you should decide what quantity a shot will be at your home bar. This does not mean that if someone else is pouring a drink they must abide by this amount. It is simply an aid for you in making uniform drinks every time, as a cookie cutter is an aid in making a uniform cookie. Establishing a gauge on how much alcohol you are pouring is also helpful if you are asked to alter someone's drink. A guest may request their next drink be either a little "stronger" (more alcohol) or a little "weaker" (less alcohol). If you are using a consistent shot you will know how much alcohol was added to the last drink and can adjust the next drink accordingly. It must also be noted that there is a degree of responsibility when entertaining in one's home. In this day of increased liability, knowing how much alcohol you have poured in each drink will allow you to better gauge who is capable of driving and who is not. When determining the quantity of a shot in your home, the decision should be based on your taste preferences, economic factors (important when throwing a large party) and even the aforementioned legal factors. When you have made this decision you should purchase a jigger (a shot glass can be used as well) which will help in regulating this quantity of liquor. Keep in mind if you would rather not use a jigger, you can also produce a consistent quantity utilizing the free-pouring techniques explained on page 17.

Now that you have regulated the quantity of alcohol, it is time to regulate the quantity of mixers. This is the easy part, but only if you have proper-sized bar glasses. This is important because for all drinks served over ice, the bar glass regulates the amount of primary mixer added to the drink. When you pour the primary mixer, leave only enough room at the top of the glass to avoid spillage, or space enough for secondary mixers. Secondary mixers call for quantities that are easily regulated by the bartender, usually a dash or a splash. For a listing on the size specifications of various bar glasses see page 26. The mixers added to drinks which are served straight up or to any other drink which is not made in its glass cannot be regulated by the bar glass and therefore must be measured or estimated by the bartender, if only by his or her eye. It is usually fairly easy to estimate amounts for drinks served straight up. There is not very much liquid in a drink served "up," and therefore each of its mixers is usually no larger than around an ounce, or about two splashes.

The glasses you choose for your bar are not only an important component for regulating the quantity of mixers added to drinks but also important for the presentation of the drink. Have you ever gone to someone's home and they served you a Vodka and

Tonic in a huge convenience-store cup or in a beer mug? The drink does not feel the same. The appearance and feel of the glass are very important for the drink. The ingredients may be identical, but the perception is that the drink served in the proper glass is a better drink.

So now you have the proper quantities of ingredients in the correct glass. Is it ready to be served? If you were at home the answer might be yes; however, if you were at a bar the answer is a definite no. The reason is that the drink is unfinished. If a bartender forgot to add the lime to your Vodka and Tonic, you would likely recognize that the drink was served incomplete. To get the most out of your drinks at home, go the extra step and add the garnish and the straw or mixing rod. The garnish will improve the drink's flavor and augment its appearance, while the straw or mixing rod will lend its usefulness to the drink and give the drink the same legitimacy it would have if served in a bar.

STOCKING THE HOME BAR

The Perfect Cocktail divides the home bar into three different divisions, the Basic Bar, the Solid Bar, and the Complete Bar. The ingredients in the Basic Bar should adequately fulfill the basic drinking preferences of most people, but will not allow for much creativity in the drinks which can be made. The Solid Bar includes all those components listed in the Basic Bar as well as ingredients not found there, making it a step above the Basic Bar. The Solid Bar level should fulfill the drinking preferences of most people and will allow for the creation of a generous variety of mixed drinks and mixed shots. The Complete Bar includes all those components listed in both the Basic Bar and the Solid Bar sections. A bar containing this variety of contents has roughly the same stock as that of a neighborhood bar. But as with anything, quality is more important than quantity. Therefore, when purchasing for your home bar you should base your purchasing decision not simply on price but on your personal tastes and the advice of others, including those in the liquor business (i.e., bartenders, liquor store employees, etc.). Remember, although the untrained taste buds may not be able to taste the difference between a cheap or an expensive vodka in a Screwdriver, there is nothing worse than the hangover from cheap liquor.

LIQUOR

When stocking your home bar, there are several things to keep in mind, the most important of which is who you will be entertaining. If you plan to have a small group, this will limit the amount of liquor which you will need to purchase. On the other hand, if you have large parties, chances are those you will entertain will have a wide range of taste preferences and consequently you should purchase a greater quantity and diversity of liquors. Liquor is the most important component of the bar, as well as the most expensive. It should be noted that the lists below take into account established norms, not your own or your friends' drinking preferences. Therefore, you should feel free to revise these lists in order to accommodate yourself and those you entertain.

THE BASIC BAR

Vodka
Blended whiskey/bourbon
Rum (light)

THE SOLID BAR

Gin

Scotch whisky

Brandy/cognac

THE COMPLETE BAR

Canadian whisky

Irish whiskey

Rum (dark)

LIQUEUR

Although liquour is not used as much as liquor in mixed drinks, it is more popular than liquor in mixed shots. Liqueurs are also popular as after-dinner drinks, and in frappés (over shaved ice) or straight up. The following lists include the most popular liqueurs, but there are many more than what is here.

THE BASIC BAR

Triple sec

Coffee-flavored liqueur (Kahlúa*)

Amaretto

Dry vermouth

Sweet vermouth

THE SOLID BAR

Grand Marnier*

Irish cream

Crème de cassis

Sloe gin

Jägermeister*

Southern Comfort*

Crème de menthe

Sambuca

Peppermint or other flavored schnapps

THE COMPLETE BAR

Melon liqueur (Midori*)

Crème de cacao

Curaçao

Drambuie*

Hazelnut liqueur (Frangelico*)

Galliano*

Crème de banana

Ouzo

Tia Maria*

Yukon Jack*

Anisette

Bénédictine*

Campari*

*Denotes those liqueurs which are proprietary (brand-name).

WINE

When purchasing wine for your home bar you should, as with other components of the home bar, base your decisions on the popularity of individual wines among you and those you entertain. If you rarely serve wine, a small selection of white and red wines should be sufficient. If you and those you entertain enjoy and appreciate wine, you should try to acquire a diverse supply of it. Always store wine in a dark, cool, and dry place. Corked bottles should be stored on their sides to keep the cork moist. If a cork dries and shrinks, oxygen gets into the bottle, prematurely oxidizing the wine. Wine should oxidize (or "breathe") for at least ten to fifteen minutes in the glass before drinking. It will take longer for the wine to breathe in the bottle because the neck of the bottle restricts the flow of air, and the surface area of the wine is decreased when in the bottle as opposed to in a wine glass. If you taste wine just after opening the bottle and then taste the same wine after ten or fifteen minutes, even an untrained palate can notice the improved taste. If you are serving an old bottle of red wine which has been in storage for a few years, a degree of sediment will have collected at the bottom of the bottle; prior to serving, separate the wine from the sediment by pouring the wine slowly and carefully into a decanter, leaving the sediment in the bottle for disposal. A bottle of wine which has been opened but not finished should be stored in a refrigerator with its cork in place. Though opened wine will not keep for more than a few days before turning to vinegar, storing it in a refrigerator will lengthen its life. There are countless varieties of wine. The list below is not a comprehensive list, it simply contains some of the most popular varieties of wine, wines to consider when purchasing for your home bar.

THE BASIC BAR

Chardonnay (white)

Cabernet Sauvignon (red)

THE SOLID BAR

Burgundy (red)

Pinot Noir (red)

Sauvignon Blanc (white)

Chianti (red)

White Zinfandel (white)

THE COMPLETE BAR

Champagne or sparkling wine

Port or sherry (fortified wine)

BEER

Beer can be grouped in much the same way as wine. Having a few different selections of beer should satisfy most of your guests. Your bar should include a major domestic lager, a light beer, and a nonalcoholic beer. The nineties have spawned a micro-brewing trend, therefore a micro-brewed beer or an import behind your bar will satisfy that growing portion of beer drinkers who prefer a thicker, more distinct-tasting beer.

THE BASIC BAR

Lager

Light beer (lager)

Nonalcoholic beer

THE SOLID BAR

Ale

THE COMPLETE BAR

Porter

Stout

MIXERS

Mixers are an inexpensive yet important part of the home bar. They are also difficult to stock, because most are either perishable or will become flat in time after opening. Because milk and juices will not last much more than a week, these perishable mixers should be purchased only when they will be used. Remember, to avoid problems with the freshness of mixers, keep a small stock of mixers and stock up on perishables just prior to parties. Instead of stocking expensive raw ingredients, you may want to purchase more reasonably priced and time-efficient premade mixes, such as piña colada mix, which combines pineapple juice and coconut milk. The most frequently used of all mixers are tonic water, orange juice, and cola.

THE BASIC BAR

Cola

Tonic water

Orange juice

Lemon-lime soda (7-Up)

Sour mix

Lime juice

Water

Grenadine

THE SOLID BAR

Cream

Coffee

Tomato juice

Cranberry juice

Soda water

Lemon juice

Ginger ale

Milk

THE COMPLETE BAR

Pineapple juice

Ice cream

Orgeat syrup

Grapefruit juice

Strawberries or strawberry mix

Coconut milk

Bananas or banana mix

CONDIMENTS

Though condiments are not used in most drinks, they will be missed if absent in those drinks that do call for them. It should also be noted that there are many people who enjoy ingredients not called for in a "normal" recipe; for instance, don't be surprised if someone asks for horseradish in their Bloody Mary.

THE BASIC BAR

Sugar

Coarse salt

Pepper

Tabasco sauce

THE SOLID BAR

Bitters

Whipped cream

Worcestershire sauce

THE COMPLETE BAR

Horseradish

Celery salt

Grated nutmeg

GARNISHES

This part of the home bar is most often neglected. If you want your drinks to taste and look as good as those made in a bar, you should not ignore the garnishes. As with mixers, the freshness of garnishes is important.

THE BASIC BAR

Limes

Lemons

Oranges

THE SOLID BAR

Maraschino cherries

Celery stalks

Stuffed olives

THE COMPLETE BAR

Strawberries

Cinnamon sticks

Pineapple

Cocktail onions

BAR GLASSES

When purchasing bar glasses keep in mind the number of people you plan to entertain. It may be unnecessary to purchase more than a half dozen of any of the glasses below. Rocks glasses are the most often used of all bar glasses. Though it is nice to serve a given drink in its correct glass, rocks glasses are the most versatile of all glasses and if needed can be used to serve most any drink. Depending on your formality and your budget, it may also be within your protocol to purchase only one type of wineglass. If this is the case, the best all-purpose wineglass is the balloon glass. With its wide bowl and tapered rim a balloon glass can amply accommodate both white and red wine. As for the beer glasses, any one of those listed in the Basic Bar section will suffice.

THE BASIC BAR

Large rocks/Highball glass

Small rocks/Old-Fashioned glass

All-purpose wineglass (balloon)

Beer mug or pilsner glass or pint glass

Cocktail/Martini glass

Shot glass

THE SOLID BAR

Brandy snifter

Irish Coffee cup

Red wine glass

White wine glass

THE COMPLETE BAR

Collins glass

Whiskey Sour glass

Champagne flute

Cordial or pony

Margarita glass

BAR EQUIPMENT

Having the right equipment behind the bar will enable the bartender to make better drinks in a more timely manner. The proper bar equipment will also enable the bartender to make a wider variety of drinks.

THE BASIC BAR

Jigger

Can/bottle opener and corkscrew/(bartender's friend)

Shaker set

Ice bucket/cooler

Bar spoon

THE SOLID BAR

Strainer

Paring knife

Ice scoop

THE COMPLETE BAR

Electric blender

Speedpourers (if you free pour)

Other items which, though not essential to the making of drinks, will greatly aid in keeping the bar area clean, are trash cans and ashtrays (if you permit smoking). A bar works best with two trash cans, a wet trash for pouring leftover drinks into and a dry trash for napkins and other nonliquid waste. If you make sure only to pour liquids in the wet trash, it can be dumped frequently into a utility sink, base-ment toilet, or other large drain.

Fresh ice is an extremely important part of any mixed drink. All one needs to do to prove this the-ory is to add some stale, freezer-burned ice to their next drink. Ice can also be tainted in an odorous freezer. It is important that the ice you use for your home bar is fresh and has no distinct flavor. Ice in the form of cubes is best.

Though not as important as ice, the other items listed below will improve any drink. The minimal cost of these items makes it completely worthwhile to include them when stocking your home bar.

THE BASIC BAR

Ice

THE SOLID BAR

Mixing rods (small straws)
Straws

THE COMPLETE BAR

Cocktail napkins/coasters

APPENDIX 4
PLANNING AND
THROWING A
PARTY

A party is the true testing grounds for your home bar and bartending skills. When planning for a party, you must first purchase the stock for your bar. If you have a good idea of what people will be drinking, you should base your purchases on this knowledge. If you are unsure of what your guests will be drinking, you need to look at several factors which may predict their tastes. Because there are trends in drinking, the most important factor is the age of your guests. Younger guests (thirty-five and under) on the average prefer weaker drinks, beer, wine, and mild mixed drinks. Older drinkers have an inclination toward stronger drinks, often unmixed, such as Scotch on the rocks and brandy straight up. Beer is popular in all age groups.

The season or climate has a lot to do with drink preferences as well. Warm weather seems to encourage lighter drinks, like light beer, white wine, and fruity mixed drinks. As the temperature drops, drinkers move toward heavier beers, red wine, fortified wines, mixed drinks with warm ingredients such as coffee or tea, and dark liquors such as brandy. The time of day at which your party will take place is another factor in determining what drinks will be popular. A late-morning or midday party will see a strong demand for juice and vodka drinks such as the Bloody Mary or the Screwdriver. Some guests will abstain from drinking altogether at this time of day, so you should make sure there are enough mixers for nonalcoholic drinks. A late-afternoon or early-evening party will see an increased demand for white wine and mild mixed drinks, while the traditional party (8 P.M. onward) will see the greatest quantity and diversity of drinks consumed. If the party is in recognition of an anniversary, special event or holiday, guests will drink accordingly. For instance, champagne or sparkling wine will be popular on anniversaries and New Year's Eve, just as eggnog and punch is in order for a Christmas party. If you can accommodate everyone's choice of drink, the party will benefit greatly. This section will help you make your bar a success at every party.

LIQUOR

If the drinking preferences of your guests are very eccentric, you may have to pick up some special ingredients. If your guests' tastes are typical, you should be adequately covered by the Basic Bar list in Appendix 3, and will definitely be covered by the Solid Bar list. The first thing you need to do when preparing for a party is check liquor quantities on hand. Unless you want to go to the liquor store during a party, it may behoove you to purchase extra bottles of those liquors which will be most popular. Vodka is by far the most popular liquor, followed by gin. The reason vodka and gin are so popular is that they are both neutral grain spirits and therefore combine very well with any mixer. Following the neutral grain spirits in popularity are rum, whiskey, Scotch, and brandy. If you plan to purchase extra bottles of liquor, patronize a liquor store which will accept returns of unopened bottles. Always check with the liquor store at the time of purchase regarding its return policy.

WINE

There can be a wide variation in the amount of wine you will serve, depending on the nature of the party. If you are having a dinner party, plan on serving quite a lot of white and red wine. It is important to know a little bit about the difference between red and white wine. Though white wine is far more popular (approximately five times more popular) than red wine, white wine drinkers tend to be (at least in this bartender's experience) less finicky with regards to taste. The red wine drinker on average has a more discriminating taste than his or her white wine counterpart. For this reason, you can probably get by with two different white wines, while you may want to purchase several varieties of red to assure that your guests are well cared for. White wine should be served chilled and therefore kept in the refrigerator or only partially packed in ice (so as not to make the wine too cold) prior to serving (45 to 50 degrees). Reds are served at or just below room temperature. Lighter reds and rosés are served with a slight chill (55 to 65 degrees). Champagne or sparkling wine should be served cold; the temperature will act as a catalyst in forming bubbles (39 to 45 degrees). A rule of thumb for serving wine, especially at dinner parties, is that light wines (whites) should be served prior to heavier wines (reds). The old rule that white wine should be served with fish and poultry and red wine with meat is still followed, but not as strictly as in the past.

BEER

If you are having a party of fifteen or more guests, expect at least a few cases of beer to be consumed. A case or two of beer can take up a great deal of refrigerator space, so unless you have plenty of cold storage space, you will be faced with a dilemma. Kegs may or may not be the answer to this problem. A keg (technically a half barrel) is equal to approximately seven cases, while a quarter barrel (half keg) is equal to approximately three and a half cases. Though they do not take up much cold storage (they can be placed in garbage cans filled with ice), kegs may be too informal for some parties, unless a bartender is pouring the beer for the guests. Another factor not to be overlooked is that today there are many distinct taste preferences. Some people drink only light beer, others prefer premium beers such as micro-brewed or imported, and still others drink nonalcoholic. Unless the party is very large, a keg of each may be overkill. You may opt for a keg, or quarter barrel, of regular domestic beer or light beer, and cases of premium or imported beer. You should also plan to purchase nonalcoholic beer.

Beer creates a situation which requires some preparty thought, so you should make some estimates of who drinks what type of beer and how much of it. You should also figure out how much cold storage space will be available for beer at party time, remembering that there will be other items (like party food) vying for that same space. If you decide to purchase cases of beer, it's important to remember that you might need to go out for more cold beer. If you've consumed any alcohol, it's probably unwise to drive to the liquor store. You should either abstain from drinking the night of your party, ask a friend who abstains to drive you to the liquor store, or find a liquor store which will deliver in a timely fashion.

SHOTS, SHOOTERS, OR MIXED SHOTS

Depending on the theme of the party, mixed shots can be a lot of fun. Whether or not you will be able to make shots during the party will depend on your preparty planning, how efficiently you tend bar, and how busy you will be during the party. Just like bartenders who work in busy nightclubs, the most popular shots can be made prior to your night's duties.

To make a bottle of shots, simply fill a bottle (liquor bottles look the best, but any bottle will do) with the proper proportions of each ingredient of the given shot. Then place the bottle in a refrigerator until the party begins, at which time you can bury the bottle in ice, and serve to those who are interested. Two shots that are frequently premixed are Watermelons and Kamikazes. The recipe for either has equal parts of three ingredients, so fill the bottle a third with each ingredient. As with all premixed shots, unless your mix is way off, you will not be able to taste the difference. This is because a shot is small and consumed quickly. If you or those you are entertaining enjoy stronger shots, popular chilled shots are sambuca, Jägermeister, and Rumple Minze (peppermint schnapps). These bottles can be refrigerated, or chilled in a shaker with ice just prior to serving.

MIXERS

At a home party, mixers are a major component of the bar, which should create no problem. They will not hog the refrigerator or cooler during a party. If just for an evening, with the exception of milk, all mixers including juice can be kept at room temperature. When compiling a list of your guests' drinking preferences use the list not only for alcohol but the necessary mixers as well. Keep in mind some of your guests may be drinking mixers exclusively, most notably cola, diet cola, and lemon-lime soda (7-Up or Sprite). Those drinking these soft drinks will consume a greater quantity of them, so purchase accordingly.

GARNISHES

You will need fresh limes and lemons for your party. Other garnishes, including oranges, Maraschino cherries, and celery stalks, are optional. Limes are your most important garnish, and you should plan on approximately one lime for every ten guests. You should be able to get by with one lemon for about every fifty guests. Just prior to the party you should cut the fruit (refer to the section on cutting and serving garnishes, page 24). After cutting, keep the various garnishes in separate bowls in the refrigerator until you begin serving drinks, at which time they can be kept at room temperature on the bar for the remainder of the party.

GLASSES

Having enough glasses for your party is of paramount importance. For a four-hour party you should plan on at least two to three glasses per person; if you are using plastic cups, four or five per person should suffice. If you are having a very large party, you may either want to rent glasses or use plastic cups. Your decision should be based on the formality of the evening as well as your ability, if you choose glasses, to clean and recycle them. Using plastic cups is acceptable, but being short of glasses or cups is not.

The most important glasses for a party are rocks glasses, both large and small. Though not entirely appropriate for serving wine or hot drinks, rocks glasses can accommodate most any other drink, even straight-up drinks or shots if necessary.

To add a special touch to smaller parties you may want to chill glasses. Chilling glasses is easily accomplished by placing the glasses in the refrigerator or freezer prior to the party. Placed in the refrigerator, glasses should be sufficiently chilled in a couple of hours, while the freezer should do the job in less than half an hour. If you enjoy a deep frost on your glasses, run some water over the glass before putting it in the freezer. If you have not chilled any glasses prior to the party, refer to the pointers in Appendix 1 ("Serving") as a simple and quick way to chill any glass quickly.

ICE

Ice is as important as any other component of your bar. It is imperative that you have enough ice. If you make your mixed drinks correctly, you will be using quite a lot of ice, so you shouldn't worry about going overboard. A rule of thumb for a four-hour party is approximately one pound of ice per person and, as might be expected, a little more in the summer and less in the winter.

Finding a container to hold ice for drinks during the party should not be a problem. If your bar setup has a sink with two basins or tubs, using one of these tubs to store ice is your best option, otherwise a large ice bucket or a cooler will suffice. The party's back-up ice can be kept in your freezer, in a neighbor's freezer, or outside if it is cold enough.

FOOD

Don't forget food when planning for your party. Whether your food selection is as simple as chips and dip or as extensive as a catered buffet table, food is a necessity for most any party.

THE BAR SETUP

A makeshift bar can be anything from a kitchen counter to a card table or anything else with space for the bar's items at about waist height. You will want to set up all of the necessary bar supplies in an orderly and efficient manner. Add a touch of class to your bar setup by setting everything atop an attractive tablecloth. There are a few other items you should not forget. You will need a bar towel for any spills, and if you allow smoking, an ashtray is a must. Dry and wet trash receptacles will allow you to keep efficient control of the party's waste. If you mix liquid and solid waste in one trash receptacle the solid waste will cover the heavier liquid waste and you will not be able to gauge when the bag reaches its maximum weight capacity.

BARTENDING THE PARTY

Though this book is geared toward teaching you how to tend bar, there are times when doing so would be detrimental to your party. Who should tend bar depends on several factors. The first factor to take into account is the number of people you expect. If the party is indoors and you expect at least thirty guests, you should consider hiring a bartender. If the party is expected to serve a contingent of fifty or more guests, a professional bartender is a must. For indoor parties of over a hundred people, two professional bartenders are in order. The second factor to take into account when deciding who will tend the bar is the formality of the occasion. Formal parties require a professional bartender, more casual affairs leave a great deal of leeway to the host. An informal outdoor party, even a large one, may allow you to leave the bartending to your guests. A large table with all the necessary components of a bar should be sufficient and appropriate for this type of occasion. If you are thinking of bartending for your own party, before doing so you should also take into account how much time this will allow for you to interact with your guests.